Testimonials

Emails Received After the October-November
2008 Market Melt Down

I have been trading the equity markets with many different strategies for over 40 years. Terry Allen's strategies have been the most consistent money makers for me. I used them during the 2008 melt-down, to earn over 50% annualized return, while all my neighbors were crying about their losses.

— JOHN COLLINS

I wonder if you remember when I boasted to you that I was switching my wife's IRA from American Century Fund to an options account using your strategy, and that I would turn her $65,000 into 100K within a year? This morning her IRA is $103,800. If it was still in AmCentury it would be about $45,000. The spreads were always invested in SPY very similar to your original strategy/or similar to your current "Big Dripper" portfolio.

My traditional, CONSERVATIVE, retirement rollover IRA/Pension accumulated over 30 years with 40% bonds and 60% stocks is down by 36% over the same period of time, while all seven of my option portfolios have a gain of some kind.

— FRED RYLAND

Terry's Tips is an ongoing educational experience for me. The Mesa approach offers the opportunity to view the changes in the market, the effects of extreme price swings, volatility and theta and still realize a profit! This trading reality has been more valuable to me than any text. The Saturday reports are a valuable adjunct, giving a detailed view of each portfolio, analyzing the past week's performance and projecting "what-if's" for the next week/expiration month. Many thanks to Terry and his staff!

— EMORSINI

.... an extremely profitable first half of 2008, then, *Armageddon* hit in the fall — Summary of my results: My personal Option Strategy accounts lost 98.8%, My Terrys Tips Might Mesa Account GAINED 34% — incredible!

— MARK OTT

It is often said that options are to stock trading as chess is to checkers. I was looking to find the chess master amongst the checker's champs, and Terry is the one. Looking for the very smart yet understandable way to trade options? Look no further."

— PHIL WELLS

Terry's Tips makes me feel smarter than the professionals by out performing the market even during the worst down-turn in decades!

— GAVILÁN

As a result of your new Big Dripper portfolio, I've been able to make substantial gains. To date, the annualized rate of return has been just under 70%. More importantly, the wide profit range of SPY prices makes it quite suitable for the current volatile environment.

— MARK CHAPMAN

Praise for the earlier editions of *Making 36%* and *Terry's Tips* (the option newsletter that carries out the *10K Strategy*).

I would like to express my satisfaction with the 10K strategies on DIA, IWM, and SPY. I began the year with approximately $80K and thus far I have just over $150K gross (before commissions). That represents about 87% growth. I did not have all these strategies in place from the beginning of the year, but I calculate that if I did, I could have well broken the century mark in growth percentage. This performance far surpasses anything I've ever done in stocks, mutual funds and (don't remind me), investment real estate. I'm definitely planning to increase my capital allocation. I also thank you for your recommendation of thinkorswim. They are a first rate outfit.

— BRAD DUNN

After 40 years of searching for the ideal strategy for a small investor, I'm so glad I found you. My Saturday mornings are spent eagerly awaiting your weekly report. Your 10K Strategy, as applied to IWM and EEM are near perfection for extremely good returns and manageable risk.

— WAYNE WOLF, CPA

I have been a subscriber to *Terry's Tips* for almost a year. This is a unique service which includes a once-a-week commentary on how the various portfolios are doing. This is an honest commentary unlike most services which try to cover their failings with phony numbers. Terry actually discusses failures as well as successes. I am happy to report that there are many more successes than failures. I have read many books on option trading and can honestly say that I have learned more from Terry's almost off-hand teaching than all of the books.

— JIM NEEDHAM

I love your program, and have been trading it for just over a year now. I also want to thank you for my new BMW 5 series. I promised myself, (and convinced my wife) that I would buy it once I doubled my initial investment through using your program. I did it, and my new car is now on order.

— JOE P.

I was a subscriber back in the rough times we had trading back in 2004. I came back on board about 4 months ago and I have already made back 75% of what was lost back in 2004 in a full year's trading. I'm extremely glad I made the decision to come back.

— TOM LA BISSONIERE

I have been a subscriber of *Terry's Tips* for the past 5 months. Everyone should try his initial offer and get a feel for his service, web site and study the results. The service has been everything the site advertises. Terry's Tips service has exceeded all my expectations. He offers a very good service and speaking for my results, he has over-delivered.

— TOM STIDHAM

At 55 years old, I've been "playing" with the stock market for years, mostly with very limited success. The majority of my life savings is in multiple mutual funds which, as we all know, are considered superior if they (inconsistently) have returns of 10–11%. After less than six months of investing some IRA funds into two Terry's Tips portfolios, however, you've caused me to believe that I really will be able to retire on a nice income — and, hopefully, in the not too distant future. Thanks for the spectacular returns and thanks for being willing to share your knowledge and insights.

— CLIFF FRISH

Those who like to use the cliché that if it's too good to be true, it probably is, surely don't know about Terry's Tips and the *10K Strategy*! Being retired, I very much appreciate the concept of a monthly income generator that the *10K Strategy* has proven to be. Thanks for a little book that changed my life's perspective. I look forward to reading the new edition of Making 36% if for no other reason other than to savor the contented feeling I'll receive by reviewing what I was lucky enough to understand, appreciate, and benefit from when I read the first edition a year ago.

— STANLEY E. CASSEL, D.V.M.

I can't figure out why everyone isn't using calendar spreads using your method. Sometimes it seems too good to be true. My returns the past two years have been almost unbelievable. I don't even try to tell anyone about it because they wouldn't believe me.

— FRED R.

After 25+ years at this, I have seen a lot of experts come and go. I have only found two where I consistently make money by following their experience and methods; one that I have followed since the 80s in the Hogs and Bellies at the Chicago Merc, and you. Nice work!

— BOB DUPRE

.... with the market at its current lower level, that in the past it would take months and some times years to recover with stocks and mutual funds, whereas the spreads that I have using your system take a couple of weeks to recover with far less upward movement in the market. I know that with my holdings in stocks and mutual funds in the past that the most recent decline would look pretty bad on my statements. Right now, I'm way ahead of my July holdings from the market peak over 14,000. I've pulled out $25,000 to remodel my house and I'm still $50,000 up in my account after the withdrawals.

— Marc Parker

I autotrade in 2 different accounts, all your strategies. I read everything you write on Saturdays. I love your happiness thoughts and everything else. I usually do not communicate at all but I had to tell you how well my accounts with you are doing compared to everything else. You are awesome. Keep up the good work.

— Maya Jagasia

I don't know if a lot of subscribers thank you but my wife and I have watched the money that we have invested in your program grow at an alarming rate. We especially like the fact, which no other investments offer, the ability to cash out profits every month if they are earned. Cheers to you and your staff.

— Rob Slaving

I have confidence in your system...I have seen it work very well...currently I have had a first 100% gain, and am now working to diversify into more portfolios. This kind of trading is actually an "art"... I have my own field of expertise...but sadly I can only offer my great appreciation to what you do so instinctively.

— Jay Giallombardo

I started with your service about 7 months ago using three different portfolios worth $70k. Those changed of course over time, but today I am using 5 of the portfolios and the value just crossed the $100k mark (actually $101k) this morning. I consider this quite remarkable considering I have been investing for the last 25 years and have never seen consistent gains as you have shown me.

— Mark Bailey

I have a PhD in math, but make my living from computers (software). It is fair to say that during the last 25+ years I spent THOUSANDS of hours reading, learning, simulating and developing trading systems. Since I subscribed to your service, I spend most of my research time on it and I gain bigger and bigger confidence that "this is it" (for me). I learn something new from every single report. It is extremely useful for me that you don't simply list the changes to be made, but reveal the thought process behind them and discuss alternatives. I feel that these lessons will make me a better trader.

— Joseph J.

Just wanted to keep you informed of what I am doing in OIH. My profits to date are $18,322 (in 7 months) on a $34K investment using the 10K Strategy.

— Roger Adams

I am very very pleased with the performance of the portfolios. I've been interested in options for a very long time, but this seems to work more of the time and with better results. So I just keep moving more and more money from my self directed Ameritrade account to the autotrade accounts at thinkorswim.

— Justin Woddis

I am fascinated by Terry's philosophy and technique. After having suffered through several booms and many more busts with my modest, self-manage brokerage account, it's a true pleasure to be able to be invested in a vehicle that's not so directly tied to the fortunes of a single company. And while I could probably achieve this same ease-of-mind with a mutual or index fund, I would have to be happy with a far more modest gain than what I've experienced with Terry.

— Eugene Hill

I thought you might appreciate some kind words from a devoted follower of your 10K Strategy far across the Atlantic in Germany. Even though the markets have been a little bit choppy due to subprime issues and wild volatility, you continue to make money for me beyond my wildest expectations. I can only thank you for being there for me and turning my investment world into a new and rewarding experience.

As a side note, I have to admit that I have in the past spent a lot of money and time being tutored on trading options. None of these courses came close to explaining how to manipulate and adjust the given strategy as you have so expertly done in your 10K strategy literature. What I liked about your approach is that you've managed to explain your strategy in terms that the layman can understand.

— Phil Davis

Am I satisfied with Terry's Tips ? — YES, YES, YES. I'm retired so I have the time to do my own trading and I enjoy trading. When the email notices arrive I always try to get a better price — sometimes I do and sometimes I don't. The reason for doing the trades is easy to understand, the trades are easy to do and best of all, it's profitable. Who could ask for more?

— Linda Nelson

My portfolio had incurred many losses until I adopted Terry's strategies. (Two other investment newsletters) consistently lost money trading options (by betting on a positive or negative direction for the underlying). The Dr.'s strategy is the only one I have seen or tested myself that consistently produces profits, not the "hit it out of the park" profits that so many newsletter authors and advisors claim, but market beating profits that you can count on.

— Tommy Hiett

After 47 years of being very active in the market, I feel as though we found the Holy Grail. Also, I can't tell you how happy I am with Kurt at thinkorswim. He has been most helpful and a delight to work with.

— Peter J. Kuehn

I want to take some time to personally thank you. Not only thanks to you the money that I am investing is growing five times faster than before, but I have also spurred me to get informed, and I have learned a lot. I am actually finding myself able to understand and predict more and more what you will be telling us in next report.

The clarity of your explanations and the no-nonsense approach you take resonated really well with my engineering background. I loved how you talked numbers without hiding behind the lingo or the empty words. The track of record of your portfolios speaks a million words. I dare any mutual fund to beat that.

— ALESSANDRO CATORCINI

To see dozens of other testimonials about *Terry's Tips* and the *10K Strategy*, go to www.TerrysTips.com/Testimonials.

MAKING 36%

*Duffer's Guide to Breaking Par
in the Market Every Year
in Good Years and Bad*

Revised 2011 Edition

Dr. Terry F. Allen

Fuller Mountain Press
256 Fuller Mountain Road
Ferrisburgh, VT 05456

Printed in the United States

Library of Congress Control Number: 2006937199

ISBN – 9780-9776372-7-1

Although the author has extensively researched appropriate sources to ensure the accuracy and completeness of the information contained in this publication, the author and the publisher assume no responsibility for errors, inaccuracies, omissions, or any inconsistency herein.

This publication is designed to provide accurate and authoritative information in regard to the subject matter covered. It is sold with the understanding that neither the author nor the publisher is engaged in rendering legal, tax, accounting, investment, or other professional services. No such advice is intended or implied. Neither the author nor the publisher is a registered investment advisor.

Options involve risk and are not suitable for all investors. Option trading involves substantial risk. You can lose money trading options. All investors who deal with options should read and understand "Characteristics and Risks of Standardized Options." A free copy of this publication can be obtained from The Options Clearing Corporation, One North Wacker Drive, Suite 500, Chicago IL 60606. 312-322-6200.

All securities named in this publication have been included purely for purposes of illustration. No recommendations to buy, sell, or hold such securities, or any securities, is intended. Readers should use their own judgment. If advice or other expert assistance is required, the services of a competent professional should be sought.

This book is dedicated to my wife, Debbie,
the love of my life and my best friend
….and to Andrew, Floery, Heather,
Heidi, Jared, Seth, and Shannon who
somehow manage to make each day
a daring adventure.

Second, this book is dedicated to
all of us who were born to golf or play tennis,
but forced to work.

1

The man who takes up golf
to get his mind off his work
soon takes up work to
get his mind off golf.

Contents

1

It is difficult to make predictions,
especially when they involve the future.

Introduction

For many years, I have been dismayed at the dismal returns most people make with their conventional investments. I know from my 30 years of total immersion in the world of stock options that better returns are possible.

In 2002, I started publishing an Internet newsletter called *Terry's Tips*. At first, it was solely an educational site devoted to explaining the risks, rewards, and unique characteristics of options as an investment alternative. In 2003, I set up two actual brokerage accounts to carry out the option strategy that I advocated in my newsletter. Many subscribers mirrored these portfolios on their own or had their broker make trades for them through the broker's Auto-Trade program.

Over the years, additional portfolios were added to provide some diversification. Different underlying stocks or Exchange Traded Funds (ETFs) were used. In the past eight years, I have made several modifications of the basic strategy that I originally advocated. Each iteration of the strategy caused it to become more conservative.

At the beginning, the goal was to achieve annual returns of 100%. Many times we were successful. Several times, we made over 50% on the composite portfolios. Every trade I made was in an actual account for all my subscribers to see — no trades were swept under the rug. Every commission was counted at the broker's normal rate. I like to think that total transparency is an important difference between my newsletter service and many others out there. (Many newsletters tell you only about their successful portfolios, and/or don't count commissions in their published results.)

While we often made extraordinary returns, there were times when the market fell precipitously (or whipsawed wildly) and we forfeited most (or all) that we had gained over the past several months. This was particularly true in late 2008 when the market fell more than it had in 80 years — our option portfolios lost almost as much as the

1

God does not charge time spent golfing
against a man's allotted life span.

— GOLFER'S CREED

market fell. Since options are leveraged instruments, we felt fortunate that we did not do worse.

However, it was clear that a more dependable strategy was in order, one which did not have wide variations in portfolio values when the markets became unusually volatile. We changed our annual target from 100% to 36% and created a strategy that had an extremely high likelihood of achieving this more moderate target.

With one exception, we no longer use individual stocks as the underlying in the eight actual portfolios. Instead, we use broad-based ETFs such as the S&P 500 tracking stock (SPY) or the Dow Jones Industrial Average tracking stock (DIA). Options on these ETFs are not as expensive as for most individual stocks, but they are not as volatile because they are not based on the good or bad news of a single stock.

I have tried to make this an easy book to read. First, I describe the strategies I use as simply as possible, without using technical option terminology. For those of you who would like more of the technical mumbo-jumbo, Appendix A contains a short discussion of the "Greeks" as they are known in the trade.

Second, I have spiced up the sometimes weighty discussion of stock options with some of my favorite quotations on business, golf, and life (three of my favorite loves).

All I ask of you is to read the basic explanation of why the strategy works, learn how to construct a simple risk profile graph (software makes this task easy) and to understand a couple of kinds of option spreads, and most importantly, a calendar spread.

Already, I know that the word "spread" may be Greek to most people. Most of us think of a spread as the expanse of someone's belly or the land around the farmhouse, or something that goes on toast. An options spread is a little different, and I will do my best to follow Einstein's advice, and keep it as simple as it is, but not simpler.

I call my favorite options strategy the *10K Strategy*. It is not a sprint like day trading nor is it a marathon where you salt away stock and wait years for results, but something in between. While it would

1

Golf was once a rich man's sport,
but now it has millions of poor players.

be nice if the *10K Strategy* was more simple than it is, I am secretly delighted that it is a bit complex, and essentially incomprehensible to most people. Otherwise, everyone would be using it instead of naively buying stock or mutual funds as they have done for years.

Will Rogers said that everyone is ignorant, only about different subjects. When I decided to make stock options my life's work, I think I picked a subject where just about everyone was a little ignorant, and after 30 years of study, hopefully I might be a little less ignorant than most of them. In the book *Outliers*, Malcolm Gladwell reported on several success stories, including the Beatles, Bill Gates, Mozart and Tiger Woods. Gladwell concluded that it takes roughly 10,000 hours of hard practice in a chosen field to become a *master* in that field. I have paid that price. I have put in my 10,000 hours studying options, not once, but several times over the last 30 years. I welcome the opportunity to share my learning and experience with you.

This book is a modified and updated version of two other books I wrote — *Making 36%* (2007 with revised editions in 2008 and 2010) and *The Mighty Mesa* (2009). I decided to self-publish these books rather than send them off to a traditional publisher. I have been disappointed by the marketing efforts made by major houses (such as John Wiley) who have published other books I have written. I felt that this book was too important for me to hand over to someone else.

Publishing a book myself has some downsides, however. I have been totally discounted by the financial press because I have the audacity to claim possible returns that are far above what everyone "knows" is possible. I sent review copies of *Making 36%* and *Mighty Mesa Strategy* to every major financial publication (and as many minor ones as I could find) and *not one single publication would write a review.* Apparently, no one wants to take the risk that I would ultimately turn out to be a charlatan, and they would be discredited somewhere down the line.

The biggest difficulty I have had in selling this book is my credibility. I have simply promised too much. It doesn't seem to matter much

1

Golf is 90 percent mental
and 10 percent mental.

that I have actually achieved these gains, and much more, for several years. Both for myself and my *Terry'sTips* subscribers.

Now that you have found this book, I feel a tremendous responsibility to not disappoint you. If you have any questions about options, I will try to answer them; email me at **Terry@TerrysTips.com**. I am not a licensed investment advisor, so I can't offer you advice on your personal investments, but I can answer most questions concerning options. I hope you enjoy reading this book as much as I enjoyed writing it. I look forward to prospering with you.

1

The

FRONT
NINE

(Foreplay)

1

Most golfers, like most businessmen,
swat the ball with all their might and
trust more or less to luck as to the result.

— B.C. FORBES,
FOUNDER, *FORBES* MAGAZINE

HOLE 1
Flat Markets Ahead

Thomas Friedman, in *The World is Flat*,[1] explained how the entire world has become flat, and why it will continue to become flatter in the future. He could have said the same thing about stock markets.

Some of the smartest people in the world see flat markets ahead. Warren Buffet, America's most successful investor, writing in 2004, said that he expects at least 10 years of flat markets.[2]

In 2006, Robert Arnott said "15 years from now, stock prices won't be materially higher than they are today."[3]

Value Line predicts three to five years of flat markets.[4] One of the most accurate of all long-term market-timing models is the one based on projections from analysts at *Value Line* for price changes over the next three to five years for the 1,700+ stocks they monitor. While their short-term forecasts have not been particularly accurate, their longer-term predictions have been remarkably on the money for over 30 years.

When *Value Line* predicts lower or flat markets in three to five years, we all should take notice.

Some observers see a slightly better scenario than a flat market. John Bogle, founder of the Vanguard and one of the most respected professionals in the financial world, makes a sound argument that future stock market returns will average about 7% rather than the 10%+ plus returns of the last 50 years or so. His argument is based on the fact that much of the past gains came about because average P/E ratios rose over that time period, and we cannot assume that they will continue to rise. In fact, he argues that these ratios are more likely to fall than they are to go up even further.[5]

John Bogle found support for this forecast from other substantial sources — "When Henry McVey, market strategist for Morgan Stanley, polled the chief financial officers of the 100 largest corporations in the United States, they expected a future return on stocks of only 6.6 percent."

1

When I die, bury me on the golf course
so my husband will visit.

— AUTHOR UNKNOWN

$$

12

Bogle also quotes Gary P. Brison, former president of UBS Investment Management — "Today's investment market fundamentals and financial variables clearly suggest that future real returns are unlikely to be greater than 4.5 or 5.0 percent."

So let's face it. Markets are likely to be flat, or at best, moderately higher for the next several years. How will you cope with this new reality? Where will you put your money? One thing is certain — what has worked in the past will surely not work in the future. You can't just buy the market and hope prices will go up. Anyone who owned stocks or mutual funds in the fall of 2008 knows this very well, as they saw their net worth fall by 40% from what it was just one year earlier.

In this little book, I will explain an options strategy where maximum gains come in flat markets. In fact, I will prove mathematically that if the market stays absolutely flat, the strategy could make over 100% a year. Then I will show how it can dependably make 36% every year even when the market fluctuates up and down as we all know it is likely to do.

1. Thomas L Friedman, *The World is Flat: A Brief History of the Twenty-First Century* (New York: Farrar, Straus and Giroux, 2005)
2. Quoted by Rich Karlgaard, *Forbes,* October 4, 2004.
3. Robert D. Arnott, chairman of Research Affiliates (*New York Times,* October 1, 2006 article by Paul J. Lim).
4. Mark Hulbert, *New York Times,* July 18, 2004.
5. Bogle, John C., The Little Book of Common Sense Investing (John Wiley & Sons, 2007).

1

Individuals should not be buying individual stocks.
They should assume that the information and advice
they receive regarding individual stocks are stale and,
to a large degree, already incorporated in stock prices.

— DAN REINGOLD,
CONFESSIONS OF A WALL STREET ANALYST

HOLE 2
Don't Buy Individual Stocks

When most people think about investing, I suspect their first thoughts usually focus on individual stocks or mutual funds. Of course, there are many other possible places to lose your money, such as bonds, real estate, or a business of your own, but these are minor alternatives compared to the gigantic world of stocks and mutual funds.

I also suspect that most people would not even think of stock options as a viable investment alternative, and since you have picked up this book, that means that you are one giant step ahead of most everyone else. Congratulations! But first, let's take a look at buying stocks.

Some reasons why a stock price might fall:

- An analyst down-grades the stock.
- The company fails to meet expected quarterly earnings.
- The company achieves expected earnings but fails to meet the "whisper" numbers.
- The company meets the "whisper" earnings number but falls short of sales expectations.
- The company meets the "whisper" numbers but issues a gloomy outlook for the future.
- The company gets hit with a lawsuit.
- The company is accused of corporate shenanigans:
  — Cooking the books
  — Back-dating management stock options grants
  — Selling unsafe products (and knowing about them)
  — Patent infringement
  — Etc.
- The company loses a big contract to a competitor.
- The market as a whole falls, taking down most stocks with it.

1

*Trying to pick your own stocks is like
trying to do your own appendectomy.*

— STEVE RATTNER (INVESTMENT BANKER)

If you own stock in an individual company, any of the above things (and many more) can happen to your stock at any time. And probably ruin your day.

When you own an individual stock, you are sitting on a financial time bomb.

On the other hand, if you own a broad-based Exchange Traded Fund (ETF) like the S&P 500 SPDRS (SPY), the Dow Jones Industrial Average (DIA) or the Russell 2000 small cap (IWM), you only have to worry about a general market decline. If this happens, you will be moaning along with everyone else.

No one likes a falling stock portfolio. But it is a whole lot less painful when everyone else is in the same boat.

The bottom line is that owning an individual stock is almost as bad an idea as buying a full-load mutual fund (see the next chapter). You might get lucky and make some money, but most of the time you will not beat the market averages.

If you insist on buying individual stocks regardless of the miserable odds of being successful, there is an options strategy that works better than the outright purchase of the stock. I call it the *Shoot Strategy* (as in shoot for the stars). If the stock goes up, the strategy will result in far greater percentage gains than if you had bought the stock instead. And if the stock stays flat, you might make a small profit — something you wouldn't make if you just owned the stock.

In November 2007 we set up a demonstration of the *Shoot Strategy* for *Terry's Tips* subscribers. We selected 5 different companies and set up actual $5000 accounts for each. Over the next two years, markets in general were awful — the S&P 500 and Dow Jones Industrial Average both lost over 25% while our *Shoot Strategy* composite portfolios managed to eke out a 3% gain. You can read all about the *Shoot Strategy* in Appendix E.

1

By day we write about "Six Funds to Buy NOW!"...
By night, we invest in sensible index funds.
Unfortunately, pro-index fund stories
don't sell magazines.

— ANONYMOUS *FORTUNE* MAGAZINE WRITER

$$

18

Never Buy a Mutual Fund

Why would anyone put his or her hard-earned money into an investment that has a 75% chance of losing?

Charles Ellis in *Winning the Loser's Game* reports that — "The historical record is that on a cumulative basis, over three-quarters of professionally managed funds *under*performed the S&P 500 Stock Average...over the past 50 years, mutual funds have lost 180 basis points — compounded annually — compared to the S&P 500."

He continues, "Even more disconcerting... the average mutual fund investor gets a return that is significantly below the return of the average mutual fund. From 1984 to 1995 the investors' shortfall was a stunning 6% annually, almost one-half of the 12.3% 'earned' by the average equity mutual fund,... The reason: frequent trading or turnover. Instead of staying the course with their investments, many investors tried to time the market, holding a fund for less than three years before selling and buying something else."[1]

How would you make out if you only bought the highest-ranking mutual funds? *Morningstar* is the most respected source — each year they rank all the mutual funds from one-star (the worst) to five-stars (the best). If you purchased only five-star rated funds, you would find that in the following year, **over 50% of those funds would underperform the S&P 500**. Regression to the mean is a much more powerful likelihood than a continuation of the exceptional returns for the prior year.[2]

Jack Bogle is considered to be the father of the index fund industry. He is known as the man who left over $20 billion on the table when he set up the Vanguard Group as a "mutual" rather than taking it public or owning it outright himself (which he could have done). He criticizes the financial industry for "telling everyone that they can do better than average, even after paying fees and transactions costs to support the lavish incomes of brokers and fund managers."[3]

1

*In my opinion, investing in a diversified
portfolio of mutual funds ranks among
the worst possible investments.*

— ROBERT KIYOSAKI,
CO-AUTHOR, *RICH DAD, POOR DAD*

If mutual fund managers really can't outperform the market, why do we pay them so much? Year after year, millions of investors pay mutual fund managers billions of dollars to underperform the market. It's one of the investment world's strangest mysteries. Does it make sense to you?

Jack Bogle and Charley Ellis are not alone in recommending index funds —

- Warren Buffet said in his *Berkshire Hathaway Annual Report* in 1996, "Most investors...will find that the best way to own common stocks is through an index fund that charges minimal fees."
- "Most individual investors would be better off in an index mutual fund." — Peter Lynch
- "Most of my investments are in equity index funds." — William F. Sharpe, Nobel Laureate in Economics, 1990
- Even a famous stock broker agrees; "Most of the mutual fund investments I have are index funds, approximately 75%." — Charles R. Schwab

A $10,000 investment in 1982 in an index fund matching the S&P 500 grew to $109,000 by the end of 2002, while an identical investment in the average managed stock fund would have grown to $63,600. The reason: While the S&P 500 returned 12.7% a year, costs reduced the average stock fund's annual return to 9.7%.[4]

What further proof do you need that non-index mutual funds are one of the worst places to put your money? Yet I'll bet that most golfers own mutual funds.

As Charley Ellis points out, "Las Vegas is busy every day, so we know that not everyone is rational."

1. Charles D. Ellis, *Winning the Loser's Game*, McGraw-Hill, 2002.
2. Ibid
3. Weekend Interview with Jack Bogle, *Wall Street Journal*, September 2–3, 2006.
4. Ibid

1

*Don't gamble! Take all your savings
and buy some good stock and hold it
until it goes up, then sell it.
If it don't go up, don't buy it.*

— MARK TWAIN

HOLE 4

Winning the Loser's Game

D r. Simon Ramo, writing in *Extraordinary Tennis for the Ordinary Tennis Player,*[1] said that in professional tennis, about 80% of points resulted from winning shots, while in amateur tennis, about 80% of points were the result of one player making a mistake.

Professional tennis is a winner's game, while amateur tennis (and golf) is a loser's game.

My graduate school classmate, Charley Ellis, in his delightful and valuable investment guide, *Winning the Loser's Game,* extended Ramo's observation to the investment world: "Likewise, the 'money game' we call investment management has evolved in recent decades from a winner's game to a loser's game... In just 40 years the market activities of the investing institutions shifted from only 10% of total public transactions to an overwhelming 90%... No longer was the active investment manager competing with cautious custodians or amateurs who were out of touch with the market: Now he or she was competing with other experts in a loser's game where the secret to winning is to lose less than the others lose."[2]

Amateur golf is also a loser's game. As Tommy Armour said in his book *How to Play Your Best Golf All the Time* says: "The best way to win is by making fewer bad shots."[3] Rather than exerting supreme effort to hit the perfect golf shot, the amateur golfer is a whole lot better off working toward consistency and avoidance of bad shots.

In this little book, I will show you a simple system using options that will allow you to win the loser's game by increasing your odds of investment success. When you buy a stock, your odds of winning are a little better than 50% (since most stocks eventually go up).

Once you understand how my options strategies work and put them to work, you considerably increase your odds of winning the loser's game. Not only will you make greater gains when the stock goes up, but you will also prosper if the stock stays absolutely flat, and you can also gain if the stock falls (as long as it doesn't fall too much).

You don't own stocks.

Stocks own you.

— TONY BALIS,
FOUNDER, WWW.HUMANITY.ORG

In this book, I appreciate that I am asking you to take a great leap of faith. I have taken the position that my option strategies have *less* risk than conventional stock and mutual fund investments, and at the same time, can be expected to generate profits which are two or three times greater than those "normal" investments. I understand that such a statement is contrary to the basic principle of investing that risk and reward are correlated — high-potential return means high risk, and low-potential return generally means a lower risk is taken.

I believe that you can win the loser's game while the professionals cannot. The big guys can't even play this game. They need to place hundreds of millions of dollars for their clients. There is not enough liquidity in the option markets for their purposes.

There is, however, sufficient liquidity in the option markets to invest $100,000 or more. I have had $2 million invested many times in option strategies similar to the *10K Strategy* without incurring any problems with liquidity.

There seems to be a niche in the options market for winning the loser's game — a niche too small for the big guys but plenty big enough for you and me.

1. Simon Ramo, *Extraordinary Tennis for the Ordinary Tennis Player,* (New York: Crown Publishers, 1977).
2. Charles D. Ellis, *Winning the Loser's Game,* (New York: McGraw-Hill, 2002).
3. Tommy Armour, *How to Play Your Best Golf All the Time,* (New York: Simon & Schuster, 1971).

1

Only dead fish swim with the stream.

— Anon.

HOLE 5
Something to Think About

Have you ever thought about who is on the other side of any trade you make in the market?

Professional investors — financial institutions, mutual funds, investment banks, hedge funds, etc. — collectively account for about 90% of stock market volume.[1] These are the real professionals. They have more resources, more access to inside information, more money than you, and their decisions are made by the brightest, best-paid, full-time and highly-educated people that money can buy.

Every time you make a trade in the market, the chances are about nine out of ten that the other side of the transaction is taken by one of these smart professionals who has all the resources that you are lacking.

So if you are buying, they are selling. If you are selling, they are buying. Just think about that for a minute.

When you buy a stock, it is usually because you have just read an article or two about the company, or received a tip from a friend or broker. When a professional buys a stock, it is usually after extraordinary research, including talking with top management of the company (and top management of competitors), monitoring supply chain and industry developments, attending trade association meetings, tracing inventory trends, and consulting economists, industry specialists, securities analysts and other experts.

Just because the professionals do 20 times as much research as you do before making an investment decision doesn't mean they will always be right and you will be wrong. But who do you think has the better odds of being right?

You can easily select the absolute best car to buy, but if you pay too much, it really is not a good deal. The same is true for stocks, and the person who is selling you the stock knows a whole lot more about it than you do. Just think about that next time you buy or sell a stock.

1

As they say in poker, "If you've been in the game 30 minutes and you don't know who the patsy is, you're the patsy."

— WARREN BUFFETT

How Smart are Individual Investors?

How smart are non-professional individuals when it comes to making investment decisions? They may not be perfect, but at least they are consistent. When it comes to the best time to get in or get out, ordinary investors have collectively been dead wrong every time.

One of the best indicators as to which way the market is headed is to look at what individual investors are doing, and do just the opposite. The supporting facts are overwhelming.

When stocks were cheap in 1990, individuals invested only $18 billion in equity funds. In 1999 and 2000 when they were extremely over-valued, they poured $420 billion into equity funds only to lose about 40% over the next couple of years. What's more, they also overwhelmingly chose the highest-risk growth funds to the virtual exclusion of more conservative value-oriented funds. "While only 20 percent of their money went into risky aggressive growth funds in 1990, they poured a full 95 percent into such funds during 1999 and 2000. After the fall, when it was too late, investor purchases dried up to as little as $50 billion in 2002, when the market hit bottom."[2]

1. Charles D. Ellis, *Winning the Loser's Game,* (New York: McGraw-Hill, 2002).
2. Bogle, John C., *The Little Book of Common Sense Investing* (John Wiley & Sons, 2007).

1

To my broker — even if he has,
from time to time, made me just that.

— ANDREW TOBIAS,
THE ONLY INVESTMENT GUIDE YOU WILL EVER NEED

Doctors bury their mistakes.
Brokers just take a second commission.

— UNKNOWN

HOLE 6
Pity Your Broker

The poor sucker just doesn't know. He is trying his best to make you happy and keep his job, but it is all a crap shoot. He knows all too well that he just doesn't know. And yet he is required to pretend that he does.

Sounds like an ulcer-producing job to me.

Remember that your broker does not make money *for* you — he makes it *from* you.

Your broker depends on his firm's analysts for investment ideas. Of course, the analysts are generally a bunch of lemmings who don't know either. If their ratings are consistent with most of the other analysts, they are playing it safe. They will probably keep their jobs.

Your broker loves it when you bring a stock to him. He can tell you that the stock is not on his firm's "Buy" list, but he secretly hopes you will buy it anyway so he makes a commission and it was your idea. You have let him (and his analysts) off the hook. He loves you. Good work!

Your broker will most certainly never tell you about trading options. Some reasons:

- He doesn't know anything about option trading (for years, I have been dismayed by the utter lack of understanding that most brokers have about options — no matter how educated or experienced they might be).
- Commission rates at full-service brokers are too high for you to make money trading options, especially the kind of spreads I recommend (each spread involves two commissions).
- Everyone "knows" that options are extremely risky. Since most options expire worthless, option traders must be losing their shirts. If he recommends options to you, and you lose money, you may sue him. He wants to keep his job.

\$

31

1

*Wall Street, with its army of brokers,
analysts, and advisers funneling trillions
of dollars into mutual funds,
hedge funds, and private equity funds,
is an elaborate fraud.*

— Michael Lewis

Your broker is probably a really nice guy. He may even be your favorite golfing buddy. Don't embarrass him by showing him this book. He will tell you that it is a bunch of crap. If enough people start trading *10K Strategy* he will be out of a job. This book is a threat to his very existence.

1

Estimates of security analysts aren't much better than those which would be attained by simple extrapolation of past trends.

— BURTON MALKIEL

Ignore the Analysts

If 20 out of 22 analysts rate XYZ a "buy" or a "strong buy," that is probably an excellent reason to *sell* the stock.

Most of those analysts' clients have already bought the stock. They did it when the analyst first made his or her recommendation. There may not be many people left to buy the stock.

On the other hand, if an analyst downgrades the stock, all hell breaks loose. If 20 out of 22 analysts have already put out a "buy" recommendation, the odds are ten to one that any change in their assessment will be on the downside. And downgrades kill a stock.

A couple of years ago, I searched for a stock that was likely to be a real dog. I wanted to find a company that had a very good chance of falling, or at least was very unlikely to go up. My goal was to set up an options strategy that would make 100% a year if the stock stayed flat (or fell by any amount). It is a relatively easy thing to do, actually, if the stock behaves as you expect, but that is another story.

I found a stock that almost every analyst just hated. In one magazine article, several analysts were asked to select their single best short sale candidate. Two of them selected this same company — Dillard Department Stores (DDS). One analyst explained that "Dillard can't compete with K-Mart or Wal-Mart on price, or get the margins of more upscale stores." While most analysts rank companies as *strong buy, buy,* or *hold* (which is generally a euphemism for *sell*), an amazing 70% of analysts rated DDS as *sell* or *strong sell*. I had never seen such a universal condemnation of a company like this.

Surely, Dillard was the dog of all dogs, just what I was looking for. Even its stock symbol reminded me of a root canal.

Over the next eight months, while the market in general *fell* by 8%, DDS *went up* by 50%. A year later, it was 100% higher than when the analysts picked it as their favorite short sale candidate. My option strategy using the stock also suffered until I bit the bullet and closed it down.

1

There should be some professional exam for analysts.
Most of the time they talk through their backsides.

— ALAN SUGAR,
FOUNDER, AMSTRAD ELECTRONICS COMPANY

I learned my lesson. Next time I find a stock that is so universally hated by the experts, I am more likely to buy it than sell it. But as you know, I don't think that buying (or selling) stock in individual companies is a very good idea in any event. I far prefer an option strategy that makes money even if the underlying stock goes down.

1

There is only one success — to be able
to spend your life in your own way.

— CHRISTOPHER MORLEY

$$

38

HOLE 8
About The Author

My name is Terry Allen. I am an options addict. I am old enough to collect Social Security, and I continue to trade options every day. I have traded options ever since they were "invented" in 1973. When I am not trading options, I am thinking about them. I even dream about options.

Along the way, I got an MBA from the Harvard Business School. A few years later I earned a Doctorate in Business Administration at the University of Virginia. While at Virginia, I lived in the computer lab, trying out various option strategies.

At the time, the publicly-traded options industry was just starting and option prices were quite inefficient. I created a computer model to help me make trading decisions. It was easy to make huge profits. I doubled my money every six months for two years while I was still a doctoral student.

Then I headed for Chicago. I leased a seat on the Chicago Board Options Exchange (CBOE) and traded on the floor. Then a couple of math professors named Black and Scholes developed and published a computer model that told everyone what option prices should be. (They later earned a Nobel Prize for their work.)

Their model was very much like the one I had created. It killed my golden goose. To this day, the Black-Scholes model (or one similar to it) is used by nearly all professional option traders. Option prices are now quite efficient. It is a much greater challenge to make extraordinary profits. But it is still possible.

In many years, I doubled my money trading options, but the most important years were those when I lost money. Those were the times when I really learned something. In fact, I would be suspicious of any options "expert" who has never had a bad year. He probably hasn't been in the business long enough to appreciate the deeper risks of option trading.

1

If you wish to know the road up the mountain,
ask the man who goes back and forth on it.

— ZENRIN

My early success spoiled me. I believed that if I didn't make at least 100% every year, I was failing. It was not until recently that I altered my strategy so that I could pursue a more reasonable annual profit goal and have an extremely high likelihood of achieving it.

Trading options has been good to me. In the late 1990s, I set a goal of giving away an average of $1000 every day for the rest of my life to worthy Vermont charities. I built a swimming pool for the Burlington Boys & Girls Club. I have provided several hundred thousands of dollars in college scholarships for low-income Vermonters and single parents. So far, I have given away over $2,000,000 to more than 50 Vermont charities.

My wife and I built a "new" 200-year-old house using materials from several houses built before 1810, and "retired" to a remote 220-acre farm in Vermont. Debbie manages some extensive award-winning perennial gardens and has written a successful book on maintaining such gardens (when we built the house, I gave her an unlimited budget for landscaping, and she managed to exceed it).

Living so far away from the rumors and noise of Wall Street insulates me from trying to form an opinion as to which way the market is headed. Fortunately, a basic premise of my options strategy is that I have no idea which way the market will move in the short run. (In the past, the biggest mistakes I made came when I thought I knew which way the market was headed.)

I rarely watch television (unless there is a ball of some sort being tossed about). When the Internet becomes too much of a distraction, I retreat even further to a writing cabin deep in the woods where a wood stove keeps me warm while I reflect on option strategies.

A couple of months each year, Debbie and I go on fairly long European hikes. In 2008, for example, we completed the Wainwright coast-to-coast walk across England, some 200 miles. I can work anywhere there is an Internet connection, and the time difference makes it possible for me to be tuned into the U.S. options market at the end of our hiking day.

1

Work like you don't need the money.
Love like you've never been hurt.
Dance like nobody's watching.

— SATCHEL PAIGE

In 2001, I created **www.TerrysTips.com**, an options investment newsletter, so that I could continue my charitable endeavors. I eventually ran several actual option portfolios with differing underlying stocks and risk profiles so my subscribers could see how different strategies work over time.

In 2005, the SEC brought suit against me for providing personalized advice to subscribers without being a licensed investment advisor. They also objected to a statement on my website that they believed was misleading. While not admitting nor denying guilt, I paid a $230,000 fine and have continued my investment newsletter, now being careful not to provide individual personalized advice or make potentially misleading statements.

So when I tell you that I have developed an options strategy that just might make over 36% every year, in good years and bad, I better be pretty sure that the statement is supported by strong evidence. I know the SEC is looking over my shoulder.

My goal in this book is to teach you that strategy without your having to become an options nut like me to carry it off. I wish us both luck.

1

*Don't play for safety — it's the most
dangerous thing in the world.*

— HUGH WALPOLE

HOLE 9

Options are Less Risky Than Stock

M ost people believe that option players are extreme risk takers. After all, they purchase an asset with a very short life, and hope it skyrockets in value. Option buyers might make 500% or more if they buy the right option, just as they would do if they picked the winning horse at the track.

The waiting period to see if you're a big winner is a little longer than a horse race, but not much. In a month or two, if the stock does not go the way you guessed, you lose your entire investment. Just tear up your ticket. You picked the wrong horse.

If the stock stays flat, most option buyers lose most or all of their bet as well. No wonder people think option trading is risky. At least if you buy a stock, and it stays flat, you don't lose anything but the opportunity to have done better with another investment.

When you buy an option, it is a declining asset. It depreciates faster than a new car. It becomes worthless in a matter of months.

High-risk, high-reward — that is an investment fact embraced by most people. They believe that any system that offers the opportunity for extraordinary profits must necessarily involve an inordinately high degree of risk.

Nothing could be further from the truth when it comes to intelligent options trading.

I am reminded of the ancient story of the blind men examining an elephant — each man touched a single part of the animal, and came to an entirely different conclusion as to what it was.

Viewed as single transactions, the following two statements are undeniably true:

1) Buying stock options is extremely risky.

Options decline in value every day the stock stays flat. Most options expire absolutely worthless, and the person who bought them loses his or her entire investment.

1

When you bet on a sure thing — hedge!

— Robert Half

2) Selling stock options is even more risky.

Selling stock options, when viewed as a single transaction, is even worse. Selling an option alone is called selling naked (because that's how you feel the whole time you have that position in your account). You have the theoretical possibility of unlimited loss. You can lose many times more money than you invested. At least at the horse race, you only lose the money you bet.

No wonder people believe that stock options investing is risky. There seems to be extreme risk all around. Just like the blind men examining the elephant, they are only looking at a single part of the picture.

Since most people have not taken the time to understand stock options, they too quickly conclude that the risk level is too high for them, and put their money into a "safe" place like mutual funds. Somehow if they are paying some "expert" to pick the stocks they own, they delude themselves into believing they are investing prudently.

To my way of thinking, they are way off base.

Below is a graph of what profit or loss will accrue in five weeks at different stock price points with a typical $10,000 investment in the *10K Strategy* (solid line) compared to the purchase of 100 shares of stock when the stock price is $72 (dotted line).

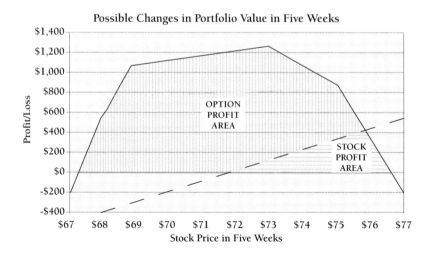

Possible Changes in Portfolio Value in Five Weeks

1

You cannot open a book
without learning something.

— CONFUCIUS

This graph clearly shows that the only way for the stock investment to make money is for the stock to go up by a healthy amount. If the stock goes down, the investment loses $100 for every dollar it falls. If the stock goes down $3 in five weeks, the *10K Strategy* still makes over 10% for the period while the stock investment loses 4%. If the stock goes up by $3, the stock investment gains 4% but the *10K Strategy* gains more than double that amount. Which investment looks less risky to you?

If your money is in a mutual fund, even if it is an index fund, these are the facts:

1) If stocks go up, you will **make money** (but your profits will be reduced by the management fees, sales fees, and expenses you incur). For the past 50 years, the stock market has gained an average of about **10% a year**. That is the most gain you should expect with your mutual fund investments. We have already seen that the average mutual fund investor has historically made only 6.3% a year. Furthermore, as we discussed earlier, most prognosticators expect lower annual returns in the future.

2) If stocks stay flat, you **lose money** (management fees and inflation reduce the value of your holdings).

3) If stocks go down in value, you **lose even more money**.

Contrast those facts with the case of a properly executed stock options strategy (such as the *10K Strategy*):

1) If the underlying stock goes up, you **make money**, often at a rate of over 36% a year.

2) If the underlying stock stays flat, you **make money**, often at a rate of over **100% a year**.

3) If the underlying stock goes down, you **may still make a profit.** Only if the stock goes down considerably in a very short time will you lose money. (Of course, your mutual fund would get clobbered in this scenario as well.)

1

*Reverse every natural instinct and do
the opposite of what you are inclined to do,
and you will probably come very close
to having a perfect golf swing.*

— BEN HOGAN

Which of the above two investments is the most risky? It seems to me that the mutual fund investment is a whole lot riskier than the stock options investment (not to mention that it yields a profit of only about one-sixth what the stock option portfolio might gain).

Why then does stock option investing get such a bad rap on the risk issue? People look at only a single part of the picture (buying or selling options) and ignore the total picture.

They conclude that if buying options is dangerous, and selling options is even more dangerous, then option trading must be doubly dangerous. **It does not occur to most people that a system of simultaneously buying and selling options might be even less risky than owning the stock.** This is the case, but most people never take the next step and learn the entire story.

The truth is that a properly-executed stock options strategy is considerably less risky than the purchase of stock or a mutual fund. However, it takes work. You will have to learn a little about how options work, and be an active part of the investment process. You can't plunk down your money like you do with a mutual fund and passively ignore your investment (although later in this book, I will show you how you can farm out the whole job to someone else).

The fact that stock options investing takes work discourages most people from even considering such an investment. That is fine with me. When I compare my returns each year with what the mutual funds are making, I feel like a real winner. I may work a little harder, but that's a small price to pay for the returns I make.

1

The

BACK NINE

(Enjoy the game)

1

I don't want the cheese.
I just want to get out of the trap.

— SPANISH PROVERB

HOLE 10
Puts and Calls 101

Here are the bare basic definitions of puts and calls. For a more complete discussion of stock options, please check out Appendix A. If you are already familiar with the basics of puts and calls, please feel free to skip over this chapter.

Basic Call Option Definition. Buying a *call option* gives you the right (but not the obligation) to purchase 100 shares of a company's stock at a certain price (called the strike price) from the date you buy the call until the third Friday of a specific month (called the expiration date).

People buy *calls* because they hope the stock will go up, and they will make a profit, either by selling the calls at a higher price, or by exercising their option (i.e., buying the shares at the strike price when the market price is higher).

Basic Put Option Definition. Buying a *put option* gives you the right (but not the obligation) to sell 100 shares of a company's stock at a certain price (called the strike price) from the date of purchase until the third Friday of a specific month (called the expiration date).

People buy *puts* because they hope the stock will go down, and they will make a profit, either by selling the puts at a higher price, or by exercising their option (i.e., forcing the seller of the put to buy the stock at the strike price at a time when the market price is lower).

LEAPS are long-term stock options. They have at least a year of life. LEAPS is an acronym for Long-term Equity AnticiPationS. Most LEAPS expire in January, but in the past few years, additional long-term months have been offered for many underlying stocks.

Some Useful Details: Both put and call options are quoted in dollar terms (e.g., $3.50), but they actually cost 100 times the quoted amount (e.g., $350), plus an average of $1.50 commission (charged

1

*The reason the pro tells you to keep your head
down is so you can't see him laughing.*

— PHYLLIS DILLER

by my discount broker — commissions charged by other brokers may be considerably higher).

Since most stock markets go up over time, and most people invest in stock because they hope prices will rise, there is more interest and activity in *call* options than there is in *put* options.

Real World Example of Call Options

Here are some call option prices for a hypothetical XYZ company on November 1, 2010 (price of stock: $45.00):

Strike Price	Expiration Date			Terminology of Option (price of call option)
	Nov '10	Dec '10	Jan '12	
40	$5.50	$7.00	$18.50	"in-the-money" (strike price is less than stock price)
45	$2.00	$4.00	$16.00	"at-the-money" (strike price is equal to stock price)
50	$0.50	$1.00	$14.00	"out-of-the-money" (strike price is greater than stock price)

The *premium* is the price a call option buyer pays for the right to be able to buy 100 shares of a stock without actually having to shell out the money the stock would cost. The greater the time period of the option, the greater the premium.

The premium (same as the price) of an in-the-money call is composed of the *intrinsic value* and the *time premium*. (I understand that this is confusing. For in-the-money options, the option price, or premium, has a component part that is called the time premium). The intrinsic value is the difference between the stock price and the strike price. Any additional value in the option price is called the time premium. In the above example, the Dec '10 40 call is trading at $7.00. The intrinsic value is $5 ($45 stock price less 40 strike price), and the time premium is $2.

1

If you drink, don't drive.
Don't even putt.

— Dean Martin

For at-the-money and out-of-the-money calls, the entire option price is time premium. The greatest time premiums are found in at-the-money strike prices.

Call options are a way of leveraging your money. You are able to participate in any upward moves of a stock without having to put up all the money to buy the stock. However, if the stock does not go up in price, the option buyer may lose 100% of his/her investment. For this reason, buying options is considered by most people to be a risky investment.

As we will see soon, however, if you simultaneously buy and sell options, your resulting investment can be far less risky than owning stock or a mutual fund.

1

Greed is good.

— GORDON GEKKO

Decay is good.

— TERRY ALLEN

HOLE 11
Decay Rate for a Typical Option

If the price of the stock remains the same, all options become less valuable over time. This makes total sense. If you own an option that has a year to go before it expires, you would be willing to pay more for it than you would for an option that lasted only a month.

The amount that the option falls in value is called its *decay*. There are two interesting aspects of decay. First, it tends to be quite low when there is a long time until the option expires. Second, decay increases dramatically as the option moves toward the date when it expires (the expiration date).

Below is a chart for a typical 12-month call option for a $70 stock. The strike price is $70 as well. If you were to buy this call option when it had 12 months until expiration, you would pay $7.80 ($780 per option). The stock would have to go up above $77.80 before you made a profit on the option if you held it until expiration.

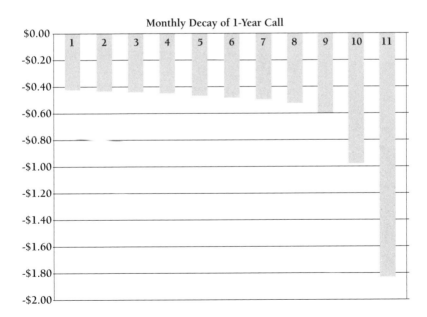

Monthly Decay of 1-Year Call

1

A good golf partner is someone who
always plays slightly worse than you.

Each month you waited to buy this option, you would pay less. The chart shows how much less the option would cost each month. If you bought the option when it only had one month to go before it expired, you would have to pay only $1.80, and the stock would only have to go up above $71.80 before you made a profit on the option.

Most option buyers prefer to pay $1.80 for an option that only has a month of remaining life rather than $7.80 for an option that has a year of life. In the *10K Strategy*, we do just the opposite.

In the *10K Strategy*, at the same time we *buy* options with several months of remaining life until expiration, we *sell* someone else an option that only has a month to go until expiration. We are allowed to use our longer-term option as collateral for the short term sale.

When you simultaneously buy a long-term option and sell a short-term option on the same underlying stock or ETF at the same strike price, you are placing what is called a *calendar spread* (also called a *time spread*). (A *diagonal spread* is similar to a *calendar spread* except that the strike prices are different for the two options.)

The price we pay is the difference in price between the two options. For example:

Buy one-year call option at 70 strike price for $7.80
Sell one-month call option at 70 strike price for $1.80
Cost of spread: $6.00 ($600)

After one month, if the price of the stock remains at $70, the price of the option we bought for $7.80 will have fallen in value by about $.40, and is then worth $7.40. However, the option we sold to someone else would be worthless since the stock price is not higher than $70 and there is no time remaining for the option.

The spread that we purchased for $6.00 is now worth $7.40. We made a gain of $1.40, or about 23% on our investment in a single month (less commissions). At that point, we would sell another one-month option for $1.80 and wait for another month to expire.

1

If you watch a game, it's fun.
If you play at it, it's recreation.
If you work at it, it's golf.

— BOB HOPE

$$$

64

If the stock remained at $70 for an entire year, and we sold a one-month option 11 more times for $1.80 a pop, we would collect $19.80 ($1980) on our original investment of $6.00 ($600), or over 300%.

The difference in the lower decay rate of the long-term option we own and the higher decay rate of the short-term option we sell is the essence of the *10K Strategy*. Everything else is just details.

Of course, this is a simplified example. Commissions would eat a little into the gains, and the stock will never stay exactly flat. Sometimes it will stay almost flat, however, and we would earn over 20% in a single month in the above example.

There are three aspects to the *10K Strategy*:

1) Place spreads similar to the above.
2) Buy "insurance" to protect against big stock moves. Like all insurance, it costs money and reduces our potential profits each month.
3) Make adjustments if there is a big price move (not always necessary).

We don't mind giving up a bit of potential profit to dramatically increase the odds that a reasonable profit will come our way no matter what the stock does.

We only need 3% a month to achieve our goal of 36% a year. The above example shows that there is a potential gain of over 20% in a single month if the stock doesn't do much. As long as the insurance and adjustment costs are less than 17% of portfolio value each month, we should make our goal. In most cases, these costs are considerably less than 17% of the portfolio value.

Endnote: You may wonder why a one-month option costs about three times as much as the average monthly cost of a one-year option. It is a matter of demand. Option buyers are risk-takers, much like lottery ticket buyers. They like to "wager" the smallest amount possible (regardless of the odds of winning), and the one-month option is their ticket of choice. Their demand pushes up the price of the shortest-term, least-expensive options. In many respects, when we employ the *10K Strategy*, we are like the house in Las Vegas, accepting wagers from the speculators, knowing that the odds are always in our favor.

1

Golf is played by twenty million mature
American men whose wives think
they are out having fun.

— JIM BISHOP

HOLE 12

Writing Covered Calls Doesn't Work

Many financial advisors and more than a dozen websites advocate writing (selling) covered calls as a sound investment strategy. Thousands of subscribers pay millions of dollars to get advice on profitable covered calls to write.

I believe they are wasting their money. Writing covered calls only limits the potential gain you might enjoy.

Let's take an example. You buy 100 shares of XYZ for $80 and write (sell) an at-the-money two-month call ($80 strike price) for $4.00. If the stock stays flat, you will earn 5% on your money for the period (plus collect a dividend if there is one). If you can do this six times a year (write a two-month call six times), you will earn 30% annually (less commissions); or so goes the promise.

(In the last chapter we showed that selling calls against a one-year option rather than stock results in a hypothetical 300% gain if the stock stays absolutely flat, or ten times the amount you could earn by writing calls against the stock.)

In this covered call-writing example, 30% is the maximum amount you can earn. No matter how high XYZ goes in price, you can never earn more than 30%. **The bottom line truth is that you will NEVER earn that 30%**. The reason is that no stock price ever stays the same.

If the stock goes up by $5 in the first 60 days, you will either lose your stock (through exercise), or more likely, you will buy back the call you wrote, paying $5, and losing $1 on the call (but making $5 on the increase in the price of the stock). So for the first 60 days, you actually made a 5% net gain ($4 net gain on a $80 stock).

Presumably, you then sell another 60-day at-the-money call (now at the $85 strike) and collect perhaps $4.25. Then the stock falls back to $80. In this time period, you gain $4.25 from selling the call but you lose $5 in stock value for a net loss of $.75.

Your gains on the calls you wrote now total $3.25 for a 120-day period (you gained $4.00 in the first 60-day period and lost $.75 in

Success is often just an idea away.

— Frank Tyger

the second). The stock is now just where it started (just what you hoped would earn you 30% for the year).

At this rate (four months of activity), your annual return will be $9.75, or 12.2% on the original $80 stock. Commissions on six sales of calls over the year will considerably reduce this return — to 10% or so. Not a bad return, but certainly not 30%. And it's an awful lot of work for a 10% return.

What is even better than writing covered calls? The *10K Strategy*, of course. This strategy is designed to make over 36% a year in good years and bad. It involves buying longer-term options and selling short-term options against them at several different strike prices.

The bottom line reason that the *10K Strategy* works so much better than writing calls — the return on investment is considerably higher when you sell a call against an investment of $800 or so (the cost of a typical LEAP) compared to selling that same call against 100 shares of stock that might cost you $8000. It's that simple.

*Golf isn't a game, it's a choice
that one makes with one's life.*

— CHARLES ROSIN

HOLE 13
Finding the Right Underlying

Stock options are derivatives. Their value is dependent upon or derived from one or more underlying assets (for our purposes, called the underlying). The derivative itself is merely a contract between two or more parties. Its value is primarily determined by fluctuations in the underlying asset.

Because derivatives are just contracts, just about anything can be used as an underlying asset, including stocks, bonds, commodities, currencies, interest rates, and market indexes.

Most derivatives are characterized by high leverage. Derivatives got a bad name a few years back when a hedge fund called Long-Term Capital Management failed spectacularly in the late 1990s, leading to a massive bailout by other major banks and investment houses. Management of the fund included Nobel prize winners, and even they couldn't understand the implications of derivatives. The fund lost $4.6 billion in 1998 in less than four months following the Russian financial crisis and became a prominent example of the risk potential in the hedge fund industry. The fund folded in early 2000.

While the *10K Strategy* can be used with the options of almost any underlying stock or ETF, there are important reasons why certain underlying stocks or ETFs are far better than others.

As we have seen, the enemy of the *10K Strategy* is volatility. Since a large gain is always made if the stock stays absolutely flat, the best choice would seem to be a stock that just doesn't move very much. And for sure, there are a lot of them out there. We all have probably owned many of them over the years.

Some stocks do fluctuate a lot, such as Apple and Google, and option prices on these stocks are considerably higher than they are for less volatile companies. However, when earnings announcements are made (or any of the other possible events mentioned earlier occur), the stock often surges or drops suddenly, and wipes out potential profits overnight.

Golf is like a love affair.
If you don't take it seriously, it's no fun;
if you do take it seriously, it breaks your heart.

— ARTHUR DALEY

The challenge is to find an underlying stock that has relatively high option premiums but is not subject to sudden price changes. The solution is not really a stock at all, but an Exchange Traded Fund (ETF) that is composed of a large number of different companies. The larger the number of companies in the ETF, the less likely a big stock price move will come about because of what happens to an individual company. However, the size of the companies in the ETF is also important — the Russell 2000 (IWM) which is made up of 2000 small-cap companies is more volatile than the Dow Jones Industrial Average tracking stock (DIA) which is made up of only 30 large companies.

Ultimately, the best underlying is a stock or ETF that fluctuates less than the Implied Volatility (IV) of the option prices. The only problem here is that there is no way of knowing in advance how much the underlying will fluctuate in the future.

You can get an idea of how much an underlying might fluctuate by checking out its historic volatility, but that is backward looking. The important thing is what will happen in the future, and as one great sage noted, "predictions are very difficult to make, especially when they involve the future."

Individual stocks are generally more volatile than ETFs, and option prices are typically higher for most individual stocks. At one point in 2009, Apple was trading at about the same price as SPY (the S&P 500 tracking stock), and a one-month at-the-money call on Apple traded at about 50% more than the same call on SPY.

Over the years, we have experimented with several different underlyings with mixed results. Google is a special case in itself. The company typically does not give much guidance to the investment community about what earnings will be, and this is cause for great uncertainty (and high option prices). Even more significant, they usually schedule their quarterly earnings announcements only one or two days before an option expiration date (the third Friday of the month). Just prior to that time, option prices go through the roof. An at-the-money put or call with only a single day of remaining life might trade

1

You can never be too rich or too thin.

— DUCHESS OF WINDSOR

for 5% or more of the price of the stock since that is how much the market anticipates the stock might move once the announcement is made.

For a couple of years, we ran a Google portfolio at *Terry's Tips* with interesting results. We usually did pretty well in the two out of three months that did not include an earnings announcement, but in that third month, the stock was so turbulent (often moving more than 5% on a single day) that we lost everything (or more) than we had gained in the other two months. We closed down the portfolio because of the huge monthly swings in value even though we had made some decent gains over the entire lifetime of the portfolio.

A similar situation occurred with Apple. For two years in a row, we gained over 100% for the year in our Apple portfolio. However, in less than half a year, the stock climbed from $90 to $180. This wasn't so bad because we started out each month with a bullish stance, but in the *10K Strategy* large swings in the stock price hurt portfolio values even if they are in the direction you are betting.

When Apple fell from $180 back to $90 in less than three months our portfolio got clobbered, and we decided to no longer use Apple or (for the most part) any other individual stocks as the underlying.

You might wonder why we didn't choose a company that didn't fluctuate much in price for underlying instead of a company as volatile as Google or Apple. The answer is simple. The problem with such stable stocks is that the market recognizes that they don't fluctuate much, and the option prices are dreadfully low, so low that the strategy just doesn't work.

Some ETFs fluctuate nearly as much as individual stocks. In 2004, we suffered large losses in the NASDAQ 100 tracking stock (QQQQ) when this stock simply fluctuated far more than the option prices could tolerate. We have continued to follow QQQQ over the years since that time, and it continues to follow the same pattern.

We have concluded that QQQQ is not a suitable underlying for our strategy. In fact, we suspect better gains could have been made by buying short-term options on QQQQ rather than selling them as

1

*Wealth — any income that is at least
one hundred dollars more a year
than the income of one's wife's
sister's husband.*

— H.L. MENCKEN

our strategy dictates. But buying options is not our game, and we will leave it to others who are smarter or luckier than we are to play.

Another ETF that did not work out because of excessive volatility was the Emerging Markets ETF (EEM) which consists of larger companies in over 20 emerging countries with a concentration in BRIC (Brazil, Russia, India, and China). We thought that adding a portfolio based on Emerging Markets would provide some international diversification from the domestic nature of our other portfolios, but we were reminded that volatility is the major enemy, and not the direction of the price changes.

After kicking the tires of many ETFs over the years, we have settled on two favorites — the S&P 500 (SPY), and the Dow Jones Industrial Average tracking stock (DIA).

SPY and DIA have many characteristics that make them particularly attractive as underlyings. The options are actively traded and quite liquid, and strikes are available at every dollar increment so we can fine-tune our risk level more precisely than for other stocks or ETFs that might only trade at $5 increments Even more importantly, there are small differences between bid and asked prices for the options, so you don't pay a huge transaction cost when buying or selling.

Another advantage of these two ETFs is that starting in 2008, quarterly options that expire at or near the end of the month are available in December, March, June, and September in addition to the regular option series for those months that expire on the third Friday. Since the *10K Strategy* usually makes the greatest gains in the last few days of an expiration period, these quarterly options provide four extra opportunities for maximum gains each year.

1

To change one's life: Start immediately.
Do it flamboyantly. No exceptions.

— WILLIAM JAMES

Setting Up the 10K Strategy

In the last week of March 2009 our team at *Terry's Tips* created a new portfolio which we called *Boomer's Revenge*. It was set up especially for Baby Boomers who had suffered extraordinary losses in their retirement. At the time, I posted this statement on the website — "**My goal is to recover the 40% or 50% you lost over the last year, and to do it in less than 3 years.** It will require that you consider an unconventional investment idea that I feel confident you have never been told about before. Nor will you have read about it in the financial press, or *Money* magazine, or in the *AARP* magazine."

As you might expect, I exceeded this goal by quite a margin. But that is another story we will get back to later. In this chapter, I want to show you exactly how we set up this portfolio so that maybe you can do it yourself with your own choice of an underlying stock or ETF.

The *Boomer's Revenge* portfolio was established on March 24, 2009 using the S&P 500 tracking stock SPY as the underlying. At the time, SPY was trading at $82.

The following risk profile graph shows how the portfolio would perform over the next 3½ weeks when the April options expired.

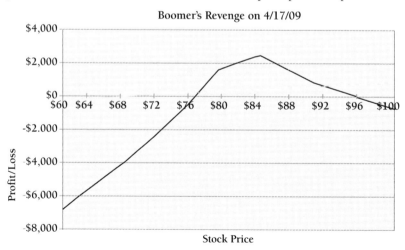

1

Anyone who lives within their means
suffers from a lack of imagination.

— OSCAR WILDE

You can see from the graph that a gain will result if SPY ends up anywhere from about $77 to $96. If it stays flat or edges up a few dollars, a gain of 15% or more might come our way. This risk profile is very close to what we try to establish at the beginning of each expiration month — a loss situation is not encountered until the stock has fallen at least 5%, and it can go up by more than 5% and a nice gain will result anywhere inside that range of possible stock prices.

These are the positions we created to set up this $10,000 portfolio:

#	Option		Strike	Symbol	Price	Total
-3	Apr-09	C	80	SZCDB	$4.13	($1,238)
-2	Apr-09	C	83	SZCDE	$2.46	($491)
-4	Apr-09	C	85	SZCDG	$1.62	($646)
5	Dec-10	C	80	CYULB	$14.28	$7,138
4	Dec-10	C	85	CYULG	$11.90	$4,760
					Cash	$477
	Total Account Value					**$10,000**

The long positions (the call options we bought) were due to expire on the third Friday of December, 2010, so they had 21 months of remaining life. The short positions (the April calls that we sold) had less than a month of remaining life. We bought slightly more in-the-money calls (those at the 80 strike) than we did out-of-the-money calls (those at the 85 strike).

We placed the following orders to create this portfolio:

Buy to Open 3 SPY Dec-10 80 calls (CYULB)
Sell to Open 3 SPY Apr-09 80 calls (SZCDB) for a debit of $10.10 (buying a calendar spread)

Buy to Open 2 SPY Dec-10 80 calls (CYULB)
Sell to Open 2 SPY Apr-09 83 calls (SZCDE) for a debit of $11.80 (buying a diagonal spread)

1

Never keep more than 20 separate thoughts
in your mind during your swing.

— ANON.

Buy to Open 4 SPY Dec-10 85 calls (CYULG)
Sell to Open 4 SPY Apr-09 85 calls (SZCDG) for a debit of $10.30
(buying a calendar spread)

About a third of our short positions were in the money (at the 80 strike price, just below the $82 stock price), and two-thirds of the short positions were out of the money (at the 83 and 85 strike prices).

There was nothing magical about these specific prices — you could select slightly different strikes for either the long or short positions, depending on your short-term outlook for the market. At the time, we had adopted a neutral to slightly bullish outlook (which is normally the case for us since the market has tended to rise about 10% a year for over 50 years, on average). If you were more bullish, you would select more out-of-the-money strikes for your short options, and if you were more bearish, you would select more in-the-money strikes for your short options.

Using the 85-strike options as an example, the Dec-10 calls we bought for $11.90 would decay at the average rate of $.57 per month for the 21 months of their life, while the Apr-09 calls would decay by $1.62 in the next 3½ weeks as long as the stock remained under $85. The difference between these decay rates is the entire explanation of why the *10K Strategy* works. The option we own falls in value by an average of $57 per month while the option we sold to someone else falls by $162 (assuming the underlying stays flat), and the difference between those two numbers is our profit. Once the short-term option expires, we sell another option to someone else, hopefully collecting another $162 each month (or more, if the stock edges higher).

Note: When you first set up a *10K Strategy* portfolio, your total account value falls immediately (by about 3%–5%) because of the bid-asked-spread-penalty (you generally buy at the higher asked price and sell at the lower bid price), but this is usually overcome within a couple of weeks when the decay advantage has had some time to do its thing.

1

There is never just one cockroach.

— Warren Buffett

HOLE 15
Adjusting Monthly Options

Once the original positions are established in the *10K Strategy*, adjustments are required every month. Most of these adjustments occur just before the current month short options are about to expire. Other adjustments sometimes become necessary when the stock price moves too much in one direction, and you will need to buy some "insurance" to protect against a further move in that same direction.

In both cases, the key to deciding which adjustments are appropriate can be found using a risk profile graph such as the one on page 79. The team at *Terry's Tips* examines graphs like that one every day for every portfolio to see if the stock has moved dangerously close to either of the break-even points (i.e., the stock has moved up or down more than the current option positions could tolerate).

Making adjustments in the *10K Strategy* involves going through a series of what-if scenarios using the free software available at *thinkorswim* – it is the Analyze Tab on their trading platform. Once you're on that page, enter the underlying symbol in the upper left-hand box, change the P/L OPEN drop-down to P/L DAY, and move the date in the lower right-hand corner to one day after the next expiration date. Then click on the ADD SIMULATED TRADES tab, and enter the trades you want as if you were actually placing orders. The B/P Effect box shows how much cash will be required to place your orders. After entering the spreads you want, go to the RISK PROFILE tab to see the new risk profile graph based on those positions.

You can play what-if games to see what the portfolio would look like if you changed the options that you currently owned or sold to someone else. Usually this means altering the strike prices or the expiration month of the short options.

These what-if studies are exactly what I use to decide which changes I want to make to achieve my goal of a reasonable profit each month and an extremely high likelihood of making that profit.

The real test in golf and in life is not
in keeping out of the rough, but
in getting out after we are in.

— JOHN H. MOORE

As a guide to which adjustments should be made, I have established the following Adjustment Trading Rules to help in managing the positions in the *10K Strategy* portfolio:

1) When the average daily decay of the current month option (using the ask price) is less than the average daily decay of the next-month same-strike option (using the bid price), roll over to the next month by buying back the current month option and selling the next-month same-strike option.

For example, if there are 10 days remaining until the September expiration (and 38 days until the October expiration) and you are short a September 72 option (bid $.05 — asked $.10), you would calculate the average daily decay by dividing $10 ($.10 x 100) by the number of remaining days (10) to get $1.00. (The asked price is used because you would have to buy back that option if you were to roll over to the next month.)

If the October 72 option is bid $.50 — asked $.60, the average daily decay would be $50/38 days, or $1.31. Since $1.31 is higher than $1.00, it would be time to roll over to the October series. (For the October option, you would use the bid price because you would sell it if you were rolling over from September to October.)

2) On expiration Friday, buy back any in-the-money options and replace them with next-month options. Most of the time you will sell options at the same strike as those you bought back, but sometimes, the risk profile graph suggests that new calls should be sold at a higher strike (which would make your portfolio longer), or new puts at a lower strike (which would make your portfolio shorter).

3) On expiration Friday, if the stock price is within $.50 of a strike price, and your short option is out of the money, if it is a call, buy it back and sell the next month same-strike call. If your short option is a put, let the current out-of-the-money option expire worthless and wait until Monday to sell the next-month same-strike put. Stock prices tend to trade lower on the Monday following an

*If profanity had an influence on the
flight of the ball, the game of golf would
be played far better than it is.*

— HORACE G. HUTCHINSON

expiration, and better put prices can often be obtained on Monday while better call prices are usually available on Friday.

4) When the strike price of a LEAP (or other long option) becomes 6% higher or lower than the stock price, sell that long option and replace it with one at a strike price closer to the stock price, using the risk profile graphing software to help determine the best strike for your current configuration of options. (The 6% number changes to 8% for more volatile underlying stocks, i.e., those with implied volatilities of 30% or more.)

5) Sell LEAPS when they have only three months of remaining life and replace them with new longer-term options. Of course, when they only have three months of remaining life, they are not called LEAPS any longer.

"Insurance" purchases: In addition to the adjustments listed above, a small amount of cash (perhaps 5%–10% of portfolio value) should be retained for possible "insurance" purchases. An example of such a purchase would be if the stock went up strongly and has moved dangerously close to the break-even point on the risk profile graph. An insurance purchase would be to buy the next-month-out option and sell the current month option at a higher strike than the current stock price. This is a inexpensive calendar spread because there is so little time remaining for the long side — this allows you to add many spreads to provide the upside protection you need.

It doesn't matter whether you buy puts or calls at this higher strike, although it is generally better to use calls for strikes which are higher than the stock price (for upside protection) and puts for strikes that are lower than the stock price (for downside protection). The reason for this preference is that out-of-the-money options have lower absolute values and usually smaller bid-asked spreads which means that you get better prices when you trade them.

If you are using SPY as the underlying, there are four times a year when it is important to use puts rather than calls at all strikes at or

1

All things are difficult before they are easy.

— THOMAS FULLER

below the stock price. On the regular monthly expiration Friday in December, March, June, and September, there is a dividend payable on SPY. It is usually about $.50–$.60. Any in-the-money call option that has less than that amount of time premium remaining on the Thursday before those dividend dates will surely be exercised and the person short those calls will be responsible for the dividend. For this reason, going into one of those four dividend months it is preferable to buy put calendar spreads if there is a chance that the stock might end up at a higher price than the strike you are buying.

These particular spreads (where the long options have only one more month of life than the short options) are purchased because they are an inexpensive way you can add short positions at higher strikes. At expiration, the greatest gain is with those short options you have exactly at a strike price. They will expire worthless (or nearly so), and the next-month option at that same strike price will have more time premium than any other option in that monthly series.

If you do not have spare cash with which to buy this kind of "insurance," you can generate cash by selling the lowest-strike calendar spread you own (assuming the stock has moved higher) and replacing it with a higher-strike calendar spread. You also may be able to get cash by "rolling over" some of the options according to the above Trading Rules. When the stock moves strongly higher, your short options at the lowest strike prices will likely trigger a roll-over because of the average daily decay calculation.

These adjustments may seem confusing at this point. Once you have managed the *10K Strategy* for a few months, they will seem simple and routine.

Note: It is not always possible to follow the above rules precisely. Rather, they should be used as a guide for putting on and taking off positions. Short-term technical measures might cause you to deviate from these Trading Rules, or external downside events such as 9/11 would call for suspension of the 6% adjustment tactic (Rule 4) since the market almost always recovers fairly quickly from such events.

1

*Wall Street people learn nothing
and forget everything.*

— Benjamin Graham

Additional Thoughts About Making Adjustments

Adjustments are expensive. They invariably involve early rolling over (or taking off) spreads at a strike which is furthest away from the stock. It becomes even more costly when you add new calendar spreads at the other end of the spectrum, usually at strikes which are closer to the stock price — these spreads are more expensive than the ones you sold. In the end, you are buying high and selling low, and incurring commissions all over the place.

The best strategy is to avoid adjusting as much as possible to avoid these costs. As much as you would like to always be in a position where you don't care if the stock goes up or down, you would go broke making the necessary adjustments to make that possible at all times. When the market makes a big move in one direction, the odds increase that the next move will be in the opposite direction. When a reversal move does occur, it would have been best to have avoided making an adjustment, and then reversing it later.

That being said, adjustments are sometimes necessary to avoid a devastating loss in case the market continues to move in a single direction without reversing itself. When the risk profile graph shows that huge losses are imminent, an adjustment becomes necessary to ensure that you will still be around to play another day. It is hard to determine in advance exactly what mathematical parameters should dictate when this kind of adjustment needs to be made, and is often more of an intuitive decision.

Owning calendar spreads at several strikes (which is always the case in the *10K Strategy*) means that your portfolios will get longer as the market falls (and get shorter as the market rises). There are times when you must tolerate being a little longer or shorter than you would like.

The goal is to make as few adjustments as possible and still protect against a devastating loss of portfolio value. One way of doing this is to establish, and maintain, a wide range of strikes in your calendar spreads.

1

Live as if you were to die tomorrow.
Learn as if you were to live forever.

— MOHANDAS GANDHI

For most people, it would be far easier to become a *Terry's Tips* Insider and mirror (or just watch) the trades we make in our *10K Strategy* portfolios or have those trades placed in your account automatically by your broker through his Auto-Trade program.

Making Adjustments for Weekly Options

The entire process of making adjustments to a *10K Strategy* portfolio became more challenging when a dramatic new change in the options world took place in the summer of 2010. The Chicago Board Options Exchange (CBOE) offered an entirely new options series — the Weeklys (this word doesn't make it through spell check but that's the way they spell it). These options become available each Thursday and have only 8 days of remaining life, expiring a week from the next Friday.

For *Terry's Tips* subscribers, the Weeklys changed everything. While Weeklys are only available for a handful of popular stock and ETF underlyings, SPY is one of them, and that is the ETF of choice at *Terry's Tips*. No longer do you have to wait 4 or 5 weeks for a monthly expiration to come around. Now it happens every week. Four or five potential big paydays a month rather than only one.

In the last week of an option's life, it decays about half as much as it does in its final month. When the Weeklys came on the scene, we thought we had died and gone to heaven. It didn't matter that we would have to trade about three times as often as we had in the past — the opportunity for our decay-selling strategy had escalated beyond our fondest hopes.

Instead of buying LEAPS (or even shorter-term options with 5–8 months of remaining life), we shifted to buying options with only a month or two of remaining life with the intention of selling Weeklys against them. Double-digit weekly gains became possible if the underlying stock did not fluctuate wildly. Unfortunately, we found that it frequently did just that (and we lost 30% of portfolio value in a single week twice in the last half of 2010). The good news is that in

1

The lack of money is the root
of all evil.

— GEORGE BERNARD SHAW

spite of these big hits, our most popular Weekly portfolio gained over 100% after commissions in the last 4 months of the year.

By the way, commissions are absolutely horrendous when trading Weekly options. Anyone who is more concerned with commission costs than they are with bottom-line results (and believe me, there are millions of investors out there who feel this way) should not even think about trading Weeklys.

Introducing VIX: I hate to complicate this discussion even more by bringing up a new term, but every options investor should know about VIX. This is a measure of the option prices of SPY. It is a good indicator of whether option prices are "high" or "low." VIX is called the "fear index." When people become fearful, many turn to options to protect their investments (by buying puts or selling calls against their stock holdings). When this happens, option prices (and VIX) get higher.

VIX affects calendar spreads because the absolute value of longer-term options is greater than the value of shorter-term options, and when VIX falls, these longer-term options fall by a greater absolute value than the shorter options. This hurts a portfolio value made up of calendar spreads.

Of course, if VIX rises, the total portfolio value should move higher. (We generally do not worry about fluctuating VIX, since it moves both ways and gains or losses in portfolio values are usually temporary.)

Our biggest losses have come when the market moves higher and VIX falls significantly. One way of reducing the impact of this combination is to insure that the portfolio is in a bullish-leaning condition at all times. A bullish-leaning portfolio can be created by having more of the calendar spreads at strikes which are higher than the stock price than there are calendar spreads at strikes below the stock price. This way, there should be a gain to the portfolio when the stock goes up which may be great enough to offset the loss that might come about because of the falling VIX.

*People who never
get carried away should be.*

— MALCOLM FORBES

Monday Through Wednesday Adjustments: Between Monday and Wednesday, no adjustments should be made unless the stock moves by at least a dollar (this assumes that on the previous Friday, a risk profile graph was established with the maximum profit place approximately half-way between the break-even range for the following week).

If the stock does move by a dollar, there should have been sufficient cash set aside to add a new calendar spread at a strike price in the direction that the stock has moved. If a second adjustment becomes necessary, a calendar spread at the other end of the spectrum must be sold to create cash for a new spread in the direction the stock has moved.

Thursday and Friday Adjustments: Trades made during the first three days of the week are usually adjustment trades to contend with the fluctuating stock. Most of the time, this consists of using the spare cash to make the portfolio more evenly balanced between spreads at strikes above and below the stock price. On Thursdays, more choices are available. A new set of Weeklys is available, and it is possible to buy back the short Weeklys that will expire the next day and roll out to the next Weeklys, generating cash that can be used to place a new spread that can make you longer or shorter depending on where you need protection.

In general, adjustments involve moving short (Weekly) options to higher strikes if the market has gone up, or to lower strikes if the market has fallen. Vertical or diagonal spreads may get established in addition to the initial calendar spreads. Diagonal spreads come into being when the short call is sold at a higher strike than the longer-term long call covering it, or a short put is sold at a strike lower than the longer-term long put covering it.

Vertical spreads come into existence when both sides of the spread have the same expiration day. If you want your portfolio to become more bullish, you might buy a current week call at a strike $2 below the stock price and sell a current week at-the-money call. This spread

1

He who hesitates is poor.

— MEL BROOKS, THE PRODUCERS

$\mathsf{\$}$

100

can be sold for less than the intrinsic value of the spread, meaning that you are guaranteed a gain at expiration if the stock stays flat or goes up by any amount. The maximum gain for a vertical spread is the difference between the strike prices of the long and short sides of the spread.

In addition to expanding the break-even point, a second goal of the Thursday adjustments is to replace existing short options with new ones which have a higher average daily decay. For example, if the stock has moved higher, an in-the-money short call could be bought back with the cash reserve and replaced by a higher-strike call which has a greater time premium than the one being purchased, and/or a lower-strike short put could be bought back and replaced by a higher strike short put which could be done at a credit (therefore adding to the cash reserve).

The cash reserve can pretty much be depleted on Thursday while making these adjustments because on Friday, short options are rolled over to the next Weekly series, generally at a credit, and cash can once again be built up.

Problems With Upside Protection: In late 2010 and early 2011, it was easier to buy calendar spreads at strikes below the stock price and be assured that the short option decayed at a faster rate than the long option. Once you moved to strikes which were $2 or more above the stock price, it was difficult to insure that you would enjoy a decay advantage. This meant that downside protection was easier to buy than upside protection.

There are several ways of dealing with the problem of insufficient upside protection. One choice would be to buy some naked long Weekly call options at higher strikes. They are cheap when the strike is $4 away from the stock price — perhaps only $.12 or less. The risk profile graph software would show that if the stock closed exactly at that strike at expiration these calls would expire worthless. However, they actually provide better protection than that. On expiration Friday morning, if the stock is close to that strike, these calls might be

$$

101

1

Change is inevitable,
except from a vending machine.

$$

102

sold for a decent amount, turning what looks like a break-even situation into a profitable one. Of course, the problem with buying naked out-of-the-money calls is that most of the time they result as a total loss (just like most insurance premiums end up).

A second way to contend with upside protection would be to buy one-month out calls at a strike $3 or $4 above the stock price and refrain from selling the Weekly calls at that strike. The only cost of this purchase would be its decay for a week. If the stock shoots higher, the Weekly call at that strike could be sold. This is called legging into a calendar spread. If the stock stays flat or goes down, the calendar spread would never come into existence.

A third way to contend with upside protection would be to place a moderate number of calendar spreads at the $4 higher strike and tolerate the small decay loss that will result if the stock stays flat.

A fourth way to create upside protection is to create a vertical call spread. Usually this can be done so that there is a small gain if the stock remains flat, and a nice gain if it goes up by any amount. Of course, if the stock goes lower, the vertical call spread will incur a loss.

Not a Simple Strategy: It should be clear from this discussion that trading Weeklys is not an easy task that can be spelled out in advance with rigorous and unchanging Trading Rules. Rather, it is an organic process that shifts in response to changes in the stock price and the unique set of option positions in place as those changes take place, as constrained by the available cash that is on hand or can be generated by removing some positions.

1

*The highest form of ignorance is
when you reject something you don't
know anything about.*

— WAYNE DYER

$$

104

HOLE 16
Trading Options in Your IRA

Since I believe that the *10K Strategy* involves less risk than buying stock or mutual funds, I believe that trading stock options is a totally appropriate investment for your IRA.

In addition to the lower risk, there is one major financial reason to trade the *10K Strategy* in your IRA rather than a regular investment account — most of the profits are taxed as short-term capital gains.

Occasionally, you can enjoy the benefits of long-term capital gains taxation while using this strategy. When you first purchase LEAPS, they may have two or more years until they expire. If the stock moves strongly in one direction (up for call LEAPS, or down for put LEAPS), and you hold on to these LEAPS for at least one year, when you sell them, you will enjoy long-term capital gains treatment.

However, most of the profits come from the short-term options that you sell. These options go down in value from decay, and you usually buy them back for a lower price than you sold them for, or they expire worthless, and the entire proceeds of your sale is taxable as a short-term capital gain. From a tax standpoint, it might as well be ordinary income.

Another advantage to executing the *10K Strategy* in an IRA account is that you don't have to report all your option sales to the IRS like you would have to do if you traded in an ordinary brokerage account. While most brokers make it easy to download option trades so that you can easily compile a report for Schedule D, it is even easier if you don't have to do it at all.

Since most people think that stock options are risky investments, they can't fathom trading them in their IRAs. If you have read my arguments in this little book, maybe you can see that managing options with a strategy such as the *10K Strategy* might be less risky than owning stock. After all, if the stock falls a little, you can still make money with this strategy while a falling stock will always result in a loss with a traditional stock purchase.

1

All I ask is the chance to prove that
money can't make me happy.

— SPIKE MILLIGAN

\$

106

Unfortunately, many brokerage firms do not allow their customers to trade options in their IRA accounts. I believe they have this policy because they do not understand the options business, or if they do, they don't trust their customers to trade options responsibly. Even if such option trading is less risky than owning stocks or mutual funds, at this time, most brokers prohibit such activity in IRA accounts.

Fortunately, my favorite broker, who I will tell you all about in the next chapter, welcomes option trading in an IRA account.

1

First get in, then get rich,
then get respectable.

— BERNIE ECCLESTONE

HOLE 17
Find the Right Discount Broker

I f you want to trade options, you need to find an Internet-based discount broker who is options-friendly, has low commission rates, and allows option trading in your IRA. In addition, unless you want to deal with the hassle of placing all the orders yourself, the broker should have an Auto-Trade* system in place.

There are fewer than a dozen firms that meet the above requirements. I have checked them all out thoroughly. I worked with several of these firms for many years, and one of them eventually proved superior to the others on just about every possible dimension.

This Chicago brokerage firm goes by the unlikely name *thinkorswim*. You can find them att **http://www.thinkorswim.com**.

For a year and a half, (through *Terry's Tips*) I sent Trade Alerts (newsletter recommendations) to several brokers who had Auto-Trade programs. Then I discovered that *thinkorswim* consistently got better prices than any of the other brokers. Sometimes they saved my subscribers hundreds of dollars on a single trade.

I think there is a reason for their superior executions. Most online brokers place orders electronically through an automated ordering system. Unlike most on-line discount brokers, *thinkorswim* has an actual trade desk. Many of their brokers have over 20 years experience trading on the floor of the CBOE. For larger orders, such as the collective orders placed through Auto-Trade, a broker at *thinkorswim* telephones the orders directly to a specialist on the floor of an exchange (someone he probably knows personally), and often negotiates better prices than can be achieved on an electronic platform.

At *thinkorswim* you will find the best analytic software around and real-time stock and option quotes, all free. I also like their order entry

---

* Auto-Trade is a program where an investor signs a Limited Trading Authorization (LTA) with his or her broker which authorizes the broker to make trades in that account (with specific dollar limits) according to recommendations made by one or more of 50 or so newsletter publishers.

1

Day trader's prayer:
"Please, God, let me break even today.
I could really use the money."

— ROBERT QUILLEN

screen. You don't have to remember the option symbols to place an order, for example. That is a big benefit for me — I hate those gibberish symbols. Does ZYXCD really mean anything to you? And how easy would it be to enter ZXYCD and end up owning an option on a company you never heard of?

Even more important, you don't have to remember whether you are making an opening or closing trade — they keep track of it for you. Most online brokers make you figure it out for yourself, and even worse, they make you enter two separate trade orders if some of your trades are opening and others are closing.

New option traders will find that they really hold your hand while explaining how to get started at *thinkorswim*. *Thinkorswim* offers great personal service (and no extra charges for telephone orders). They will get you set up for one of their Auto-Trade portfolios without your having to enter any orders. I don't know of another broker who offers this service.

You are offered a choice of commission plans at *thinkorswim* — their own, which has lower rates for very small orders, or you can select the same commission schedule offered by several other discount brokers.

There are a few other firms who have lower commission rates, but they have serious shortcomings as well. Most of them do not have Auto-Trade programs and more importantly, they do not have a good system for handling early exercise of short options that sometimes occurs. I have a collection of horror stories sent to me by my newsletter subscribers concerning some of these brokers.

Several brokers have asked me to participate in their Auto-Trade program by sending them my Trade Alerts as they are issued. (Of course, their clients would be *Terry's Tips* Premium Service subscribers.) While I understand that my business might expand considerably if I took them up on their offers, I have decided, at least at this point, to decline their invitations.

My reasons are two-fold — first, I am reluctant to expand my staff (we are a very small and skilled team that has been together for over seven years, with every member working from his or her own home

*It isn't necessary to be rich and
famous to be happy. It's only
necessary to be rich.*

— ALAN ALDA

here in Vermont). Second, I believe that *thinkorswim* offers the absolute best package of trading platforms, free analytic software, commission rates, and executions. I suspect that participating in other brokers' Auto-Trade programs would be considered to be a tacit endorsement of that brokerage, and I am unwilling to take that risk when I am convinced that *thinkorswim* offers the best available package.

I will continue to monitor other firms to see if their service improves to match that of *thinkorswim*, and let my newsletter subscribers know if another good alternative comes along. So far, it hasn't.

Endnote: I am not alone in preferring *thinkorswim* — Barron's has voted them Best Overall Online Broker for three years running.

1

Take calculated risks.
That is quite different from being rash.

— GEORGE S. PATTON

HOLE 18
Stock Investing vs. Options Investing

I believe that stock option trading is the one arena where there is a level playing field for the individual investor and Wall Street. In fact, you can win this loser's game while the professionals cannot. The big guys can't even play. They need to place hundreds of millions of dollars for their clients. There is not enough liquidity in the option markets for their purposes.

There are probably a thousand people who buy stocks and mutual funds for every person who trades in stock options. That puts us in pretty rare company. Even better, instead of buying the cheapest options available, as most option traders do, we do just the opposite. When we use the *10K Strategy* we are essentially taking the role of the house at the casino, taking in the bets made by the lottery-ticket buyers.

There seems to be a potentially profitable niche in the options market — a niche too small for the big guys but plenty big enough for you and me. And it isn't very crowded.

The biggest differences between the world of stocks (or mutual funds) and the world of options can be explained in mathematical terms. Stocks change arithmetically and options change geometrically.

These generalizations can be made:

If your stock goes up by 2% in one month, your stock portfolio will go up by that same 2%. The same change will take place if the stock goes down. There will be a linear arithmetic relationship between stock prices and portfolio values.

If the underlying stock of your options portfolio goes up by 2%, your portfolio value might do just about anything. If you are using the *10K Strategy*, it will probably gain an average of 6%–10% for that month. It would make that same average gain if the stock stayed flat or fell by 2% as well. (The *10K Strategy* likes 2% monthly stock price changes regardless of which direction they go.)

$$$

115

1

Since the dawn of capitalism,
there has been one golden rule:
"If you want to make money,
you have to take risks."

— Announcer,
Opening line of the Nova Special,
The Trillion Dollar Bet

For those of us who love options, the arithmetic world of stocks is boring. It is like watching grass grow. Just about anything is more exciting. Even watching mind-numbing sit-coms.

Let's compare the arithmetic changes in the stock portfolio with the expected geometric changes in a *10K Strategy* portfolio. These things are true:

1) If the underlying stock stays flat or goes *up* by 1%, 2%, 3%, or 4% during one expiration month, the portfolio value should increase by an average 4%–10% after commissions.

2) If the underlying stock stays flat or goes *down* by 1%, 2%, 3%, or 4% during one expiration month, the portfolio value should increase by an average 4%–10% after commissions.

3) If the underlying stock goes up or down by 5% during one expiration month, the portfolio value will most likely break even (on average).

4) If the underlying stock goes up or down by 6% or more during one expiration month, *unless adjustments are made*, the options portfolio will lose money, and that loss could be double or more the percentage loss in the underlying stock.

5) The greater the percentage change in the underlying, the greater the possible percentage loss of the options portfolio. If the underlying stock falls by 15% in one expiration month, *unless adjustments are made*, the options portfolio could lose 40%.

It is clear from these statements that an important part of successfully operating the *10K Strategy* is to have an effective adjustment strategy ready to implement in those months where the underlying stock is more than moderately volatile. Such adjustment tactics are critical. They alone will save the investor from the geometrical changes in portfolio value that might result if the stock moves significantly and no adjustments are made. (Chapter 15 discusses adjustments.)

1

The early bird catches the worm,
but it is the second mouse who
gets the cheese.

— Unknown

If you get involved in the *10K Strategy* options strategy, some things are certain. First, you will feel lonely. Not one person in 100 will have any idea about what you are doing. You won't be able to trade war stories with your friends about the various horses (stocks) you placed your money on last week. You won't care one whit about how well a single company does.

Second, you will pay at least ten times as much as your stock-picking friends pay for commissions. But you are safe here — your friends won't know.

Third, everyone will think that you are a gun-slinging wild speculator who doesn't have any idea about prudent investments. Some of them will probably assume that you are desperate, betting your last dollar on a long shot in hopes to catch up with them and their conservative stock, bond, mutual fund, and CD "investments."

On the other hand, there are some positives to the option alternative. When the market stays flat (even though it moves up and then back down, as it usually does), your friends will not have made any money at all while you might easily have made more than they make in an entire year. This simple possibility should be reason enough to take a closer look at the *10K Strategy* alternative.

There will be times when the market tanks and your option portfolio actually makes money. Those are the most delicious times of all.

So, bottom-line, if you don't care about your friends thinking you are a loner, and an imprudent and desperate speculator, and all you care about is making extraordinary returns every year regardless of what the market does, you can jump on the options bandwagon with me.

All I ask is that you put a small amount aside, say $10,000, and give it a try for three months. At the end of that time, you will have a better idea of whether or not you are a believer or not. If even this seems too risky, you could become a *Terry's Tips* Insider and watch several actual *10K Strategy* portfolios unfold over time before you plunk down any of your precious cash.

1

You can never predict when that unknown
torpedo will come out of the dark
and smash the price of a stock.

— RALPH SEGER

A Note About Option Commissions

Commission costs are considerably higher in option trading compared to stock trading.

If you buy 100 shares of a $50 stock, you would shell out $5,000 plus about a $10 commission at your favorite discount broker. The only thing you know for certain about this purchase is that it ties up $5,010 that could be earning interest in a savings account.

A year later, unless the stock has increased in value, you still would not have covered the money you paid out for the commission. Even though the commission works out to only 0.2% of the total investment, it is no wonder that commissions are a concern for stock traders.

Contrast the stock purchase to the sale of a single option for $1.50 (a one-month at-the-money call or put option on SPY could be sold for almost double this amount, but let's take the lower number). On the $150 sale, a typical discount broker might charge a commission of $1.50. This works out to 1% of the purchase price, or 5 times the percentage you would have paid to buy the stock.

However, the option-seller has sold a depreciating asset that goes down in value every day. Over the course of the next month, the time premium of the option that was sold for $150 will depreciate by an average of $5 per day. In other words, one day after selling the option, if the stock price doesn't change, the commission cost will have been totally recovered more than 3 times over.

Of course, if a call were sold and the stock went up, the option that was sold for $1.50 might cost more to buy back the next day, but the option seller presumably owns an off-setting longer-term call that will also increase in value. But the bottom line is the same — **every single day of the short option's life, the entire commission cost will be more than covered by the lowering value (decay) of the option.**

The buyer of stock might have to wait a year or more for the stock to go up and finally cover his commission cost while the option-seller will usually cover his commission cost before lunch-time the following day.

I have spent most of my life golfing…
the rest I've just wasted.

— ANON.

In his mind, the option-seller should think of the commission cost as evidence that he has made a good investment that will pay for itself in less than a day. The more commissions you pay, the more decay you will be collecting.

This is just another example that the world of stock investing is far different from the world of option investing. While it may take a year to recover the commission you pay on a stock purchase, you would be disappointed if it took an entire day to recover that cost if you sold an option.

In spite of the extraordinary transaction costs of option trading, there are many option newsletters on the Internet that report their returns without recognizing commission costs. I can't understand how they stay in business.

It is best to think of transaction costs in an options portfolio as you would the interest costs of a commercial real estate investment. Interest might amount to 60% or more of your rental income, but if your net return was attractive, you wouldn't give the interest cost a second thought. It is only a necessary cost of owning that kind of investment.

Many people foolishly compare their commission costs in an option portfolio to the commission costs of trading stocks or mutual funds. That is a mistake. Anyone who focuses on transaction costs rather than the bottom line should not be trading options.

I believe the net gains from the *10K Strategy* should be far greater than virtually any mutual fund or real estate investment even after the extraordinarily high transaction costs are covered.

1

If you want your ship to come in,
you must build a dock.

HOLE 19
Getting Started

I have tried to make the discussion of the *10K Strategy* as non-technical and simple as possible. It has not been easy. Trying to create options positions that almost never lose money is inherently a complex challenge.

I have tried to come up with precise Trading Rules that anyone could follow, especially in the area of making adjustments. But this has proved to be impossible. Instead, I have set forth some general rules of thumb that can be acted up in conjunction with a close examination of the current risk profile graph for each portfolio. Depending on when during the expiration month (and the direction of the underlying price change), different adjustments might be called for. There are no hard and fast rules that can be applied in all situations. Even general rules of thumb can be misleading at times.

I think most readers will conclude that carrying out the *10K Strategy* is not a do-it-yourself project. It requires essentially daily attention, and most people have better things to do with their daylight hours.

The Auto-Trade Alternative

Fortunately, there is a method by which anyone can carry out the *10K Strategy* and have a life of his or her own. It is called Auto-Trade.

Auto-Trade is available at many discount brokers who specialize in options, including *thinkorswim*. In Auto-Trade, you authorize your broker to makes trades in your account based on Trade Alerts (recommendations to make a specific trade) made by any of 50 or so newsletters such as *Terry's Tips*. Before the broker will place trades for you, he contacts the newsletter and confirms that you are a paying subscriber to that newsletter.

There is no extra charge for trades made through Auto-Trade at *thinkorswim* (some brokers do charge extra, however). Since your orders are placed with many other investors as one huge order, the

1

Rise early. Work hard. Strike oil.

— J. PAUL GETTY

Sleep late. Save a little.
Create a 10K portfolio.

— TERRY ALLEN

broker can often negotiate better prices on Auto-Trade orders than an individual can get through the automated options trading system.

Getting Set Up With *Terry's Tips*

There are four different ways for you to put the *10K Strategy* to work:

1) Do it on your own.
2) Subscribe to the *Terry's Tips* Basic Service.
3) Subscribe to the *Terry's Tips* Premium Service.
4) Subscribe to both the Basic and Premium Service.

1) Do it on your own. If you want to create your own *10K* portfolio on your own, without ongoing guidance from *Terry's Tips*, you know what you need to do to get set up with your broker. I hope I have given you sufficient instructions on how to manage the strategy. At first, you may want to use a service provided by many discount brokers (including *thinkorswim*) called paper trading – it allows you to try the strategy for awhile until you get more comfortable with it without risking any real money.

2) Subscribe to the *Terry's Tips* Basic Service. If you would like to mirror one or more of our *10K* portfolios with some ongoing guidance from *Terry's Tips*, our regular subscription service involves an initial purchase of our White Paper ($79.95). This report offers a detailed description of several strategies in addition to the *10K Strategy*.

The White Paper also includes a list of 20 "Lazy Way" companies where a 100% gain is mathematically guaranteed in two years if the stock stays flat, goes up by any amount, or falls less than 5% or 10%. Most of these stocks can fall by 25% or more over the two years and a profit is also realized. It is called the "Lazy Way" strategy because only two trades are made at the beginning of the period, and then you just sit and wait it out for an average of two years. (The "Lazy Way"

The road to success is usually
off the beaten path.

— FRANK TYGER

strategy cannot be conducted in an IRA, but all the other *Terry's Tips'* portfolios can be mirrored in an IRA.)

Along with the White Paper, you will receive an Options Tutorial Program with a new lesson delivered each day for 14 days. In addition, you will receive two free months of *Insider* access. This includes our weekly reports which describe the current positions and risk profile graphs of several portfolios using several different ETFs as the underlyings.

After these two free months, you may wish to continue with our regular subscription program at the rate of $19.95 per month. The regular service includes Trade Alerts which are sent out at the end of the trading day for all the portfolios. These Trade Alerts include the specific trades which need to be made each portfolio and the prices that should be paid.

Since these alerts are sent out at the end of the day, the prices may or may not be available in the market on the next day. However, many *Terry's Tips* subscribers have successfully mirrored our portfolios with the regular subscription service.

To get set up with the regular *Terry's Tips* service, go to **www.TerrysTips.com/order/php** and check the box for the White Paper and Options Tutorial Program.

3) **Subscribe to the *Terry's Tips* Premium Service.** This alternative is designed for people who wish to have one or more *10K* portfolios managed in their own account for them through a broker's Auto-Trade program, or who need real-time notification of trades being made in *Terry's Tips* portfolios.

This is a simpler alternative. It does not involve buying the White Paper and learning all about trading options. Once you are set up with Auto-Trade, *thinkorswim* does everything for you automatically, and you can go about your everyday life without checking on the market every few hours.

1

It is not easy to get rich in Las Vegas,
at Churchill Downs or at the local
Merrill Lynch office.

— PAUL A. SAMUELSON

The Premium Service includes real-time Trade Alerts sent to you and your broker. This allows you to make trades at the actual prices that are available during the day when the alert is issued rather than waiting until the next day and hoping that those prices are still available.

The Premium Service costs $40.00 for the first month (which includes the set-up fee) and $49.98 for subsequent months unless you decide to upgrade your service and subscribe to multiple portfolios. This monthly fee is the same regardless of whether you have invested $5,000 or $1,000,000 or more. It is charged directly to your credit card and is not taken out of your broker account. (Of course, *Terry's Tips* has no access to or knowledge about your account. You are free to place other trades in this same account if you wish, as long as you leave as much cash that exists in the actual *Terry's Tips* 10K portfolio account that you will see updated each week).

If you want to proceed with this alternative, your first task is to open an account (IRA or regular) at **www.thinkorswim.com**.

If you want to withdraw cash from your account as we do in the actual *10K* portfolios at *Terry's Tips* (see Withdrawal Rules in Appendix D), you will have to initiate this withdrawal on your own. *thinkorswim* makes it easy to do online.

To get set up for the Premium Service at *Terry's Tips*, go to **www.TerrysTips.com/order/php** and check the box for Premium Service and Auto-Trade. You do not have to do this until you have set up your brokerage account, but signing up early is a quick way to see exactly how the actual *10K* portfolios are doing, and give you some time to decide which portfolio is most appropriate for you to follow.

4) **Subscribe to both the Basic and Premium Service.** This $119.95 choice gives you all the instructional materials of the Basic Service (including the $79.95 White Paper) and two free months of the Premium Service (worth $99.96). This is the best choice if you want to learn everything we offer about options investing as well as actually investing some of your own money as well.

1

Just do it!

— NIKE AD

This ends my explanation of the *10K Strategy*. The rest of the book is for those who want to delve deeper into the details of the option world. It is not easy to explain any strategy involving options. They are derivative instruments which are complex and often confusing, and that is why very few people ever get involved with them.

In spite of the inherent complexity of options, I hope I have presented a relatively understandable explanation of why I believe this strategy has a high likelihood of achieving extraordinary investment gains year after year.

I invite you to participate in this adventure with me, and I wish both of us the best of luck on our journey together.

$$$

133

1

Time is money.

— BENJAMIN FRANKLIN

Time is everything.

— NAPOLEON

I hate quotations.

— RALPH WALDO EMERSON

Appendix A
THE GREEKS AND IMPLIED VOLATILITY

The "Greeks" are measures designed to better understand how option prices change when the underlying stock changes in value and/or time passes by (and options decline in value).

My goal is to keep this discussion of Greek measures as simple as possible. It is not easy. I have tried many times to explain these terms to people in person. I have seen their eyes glaze over before I get past Alpha.

I'm sure you heard about the fellow who bragged that he could speak every language except Greek, and when asked to say something in a particular foreign language, answered "It's all Greek to me." Let's hope that isn't your answer next time you are asked about a Greek stock option measure.

I'll confine this discussion to three measures of market risk exposure — **delta, gamma**, and **theta**. Mathematicians gave these measures the names of Greek letters, or names that sound like they're Greek letters (vega, another measure which we will not discuss here, is not in the Greek alphabet, but sounds like it should be). Delta, gamma, and theta are the three most important Greeks in the world of stock options, and each tells us something important about an option.

If you own 100 shares of a company's stock, your market risk is easy to understand. If the stock rises (or falls) by $1.00, you gain (or lose) $100. It's not so simple with stock options. The most common way to measure market risk for an option is the Greek called delta.

Delta is the amount the option will change in value if the stock goes up by $1.00. If an option carries a delta of 70, and the stock goes up by $1.00, the price of the option will rise by $.70 ($70 since each option is worth 100 shares).

Owning an option that has a delta of 70 means that you own the equivalent of 70 shares of the company's stock.

All options do not have the same delta value. Deep in-the-money options have very high delta values (perhaps in the 90s), while way out-of-the-money options have very low delta values (could be under 10).

To make matters more confusing, delta values change over the life of the option, even if the price of the stock remains unchanged. An in-the-money option, which might have a delta value of 60 with a month to go until expiration, will have a delta value of essentially 100 on expiration Friday.

You can calculate the net delta value of your composite option positions by multiplying the delta value of your long options by the number of those options and subtracting the delta value of your short options multiplied by the number of those options. The resulting figure, **net delta value**, tells you how much the value of your current option portfolio will change if the underlying stock goes up by $1.00. It is perhaps the best measure of market risk at any given moment.

Most professional market makers who hold a variety of options in their account, some long, some short, some puts and some calls, calculate their net delta value continually throughout the day so that they don't expose themselves to more risk than their comfort level allows. Ideally, they like to be net delta neutral, which means that with their current configuration of option holdings, they do not care whether the market goes up or down.

Gamma is a measure of how much delta changes with a dollar change in the price of the stock. This is a more complex measure, and really shouldn't be of too much concern to you as long as you stick with the calendar spreads like those used in the *10K Strategy*.

Just as with deltas, all gammas are different for different options. While you may establish a net delta neutral position (i.e., you don't care if the stock goes up or down), the gamma will most always move you away from delta neutrality as soon as the underlying stock changes in value.

If there is a lot of time left in an option (such as a LEAP), the gamma tends to be quite stable (i.e., low). This holds true for both in-the-money and out-of-the-money options. Short-term options, on the other hand, have widely fluctuating gammas, especially when the strike price of the option is very close to the stock price.

A perfectly neutral option strategy would have a zero net delta position and a zero net gamma position. As long as you deal with calendar spreads, you will never enjoy this luxury. You will always see your net delta position fall as the stock price rises, and watch your net delta position rise as the stock price falls. Gamma measures tend to do the same, which serves to accelerate the change in the net delta position of a calendar spread portfolio.

Occasionally checking out the net gamma position lets you know how big the change in your net delta position will be if the stock moves up or down in price. It helps you know how your exposure to market risk will change as the stock price changes.

Theta is my favorite Greek, because it tells me how much money I will make today if the price of the stock stays flat. Theta is the amount of daily decay. It is expressed as a negative number if you own an option (that is how much your option will decay in value in one day).

On the other hand, if you are short an option, theta is a positive number which shows how much you will earn while the option you sold to someone else goes down in value in one day. (The *10K Strategy* essentially always has a positive net theta position, meaning that time is on your side. It tells you exactly how many dollars you will make today if the stock stays flat. For me, knowing this number has some negative implications, however. If I'm at a restaurant on a night when the market didn't change much, I might remember the theta value that day – it was sort of "free" money I really didn't make any effort to earn. Oftentimes, I order a too-expensive bottle of wine because of that silly theta number).

The ultimate goal of the *10K Strategy* is to maximize the net theta position in your account without letting the net delta value get so high or low that you will lose a lot of money if the stock moves against you.

This short discussion of the Greeks should be all you need to impress your friends next time you talk about the stock market. All you need to do is to get around to the topic of stock options, and drop a few Greek names on them (ask them if they know what their net delta position was yesterday, or did their theta increase much last week, and watch their eyes glaze over).

I have found that the Greeks are very effective conversation stoppers. Feel free to use them whenever the need arises.

Implied Volatility

Stock option prices are determined by a variety of factors. The most important are the stock price in relation to the strike price, the length of time until expiration, the interest rate (because an option saves you much of the investment required to purchase the stock), and the dividend of the stock. All of these factors are precisely measurable at any given point in time.

Yet if two different stocks have identical numbers for all of the above variables, their option prices may differ by a considerable amount. The reason is Implied Volatility (IV) of the option.

IV is the market's estimate of how much the price of the underlying stock will fluctuate in a year. It is expressed as a percentage. If an option has an IV of 30, this means the market expects the stock to fluctuate by 30% in either direction over the course of a year. IV is usually closely related to the historic volatility of the stock unless unusual events are expected for the company. (Historic volatility for all stocks which have options can be found at the www.cboe.com or on the trading screen at *thinkorswim*.)

IV is the best measure of whether option prices are "high" or "low." The higher the IV, the higher the option prices. This is true for both puts and calls.

An interesting feature of option prices is that IVs are sometimes different for different option months. IV for the current month's options tends to increase shortly before important company events such as the announcement of earnings or a rumored impending acquisition. (IVs for longer-term options do not fluctuate as much when important events are imminent.)

The *10K Strategy* does best if you can buy options with relatively low IVs and sell options with relatively high IVs. If you can find a spread where your long option has a lower IV than your short option, it clearly gives you a big edge.

I think there is a logical explanation for why the IVs for next-month options are often lower than any other option months — people are writing calls against their stock. Call-writers like rapid decay, and the next-month options provide the highest decay rates. If a large number of people are writing calls (or buying calendar spreads as the *10K Strategy* does), the prices of the short-term call options would become relatively depressed. In the case of calendar spreads, longer-term options are being purchased, pushing those option prices up (as well as their IVs).

For many companies, IVs do not escalate prior to an earnings announcement because earnings are relatively predictable. But for companies such as Apple (where quarterly earnings often fluctuate considerably) and Google (where company management doesn't tell analysts much about expected earnings), current-month option IV often skyrockets shortly before earnings announcements.

IV is an important factor in the success of the *10K Strategy*. Profits can be made with the strategy even if IV is not on your side, but you gain a huge advantage when you have it. When the IV for the short-term options (which the *10K Strategy* is short, i.e., has sold) is greater than the IV of the longer-term options (which the *10K Strategy* is long, i.e., has bought), we call this an IV Advantage. It allows you to buy relatively cheap options and sell relatively expensive options. While an IV Advantage is often difficult to find, it is worth looking for whenever you are considering a new company to trade using the *10K Strategy*.

Appendix B
WHY PUTS MAY BE BETTER THAN CALLS FOR CALENDAR SPREADS

When you think of calls, you think about hoping the stock will go up. When you think of puts, you think about hoping the stock will go down. Those thoughts are appropriate when you are buying options. But they most certainly are wrong when you are buying calendar spreads.

When buying calendar spreads (also called time spreads), the strike price tells you which way you want the stock to go, not the choice of puts or calls. You always want the stock to move toward the strike price of your calendar spreads. That is where the maximum gain will take place, regardless of whether you own puts or calls.

There are two reasons why puts may be a better choice than calls for calendar spreads:

1) The premium decay difference (the difference between the decay of the long-term options you own and the short-term options you have sold) is essentially the same for put and call spreads.
2) The put spreads often cost less than the call spreads at the same strike price.

In the graphs on the next page, I have compared the risk profile of a typical calendar spread portfolio using calls and the same calendar spreads using puts. These spreads were set up for Sears Holdings (SHLD) at the 110, 120, and 130 strikes (at a time when SHLD was trading about $119). The long positions had seven months until expiration and the short positions had two months until expiration. Note the essentially identical curves. It truly does not matter whether you are trading in puts or calls from a payoff basis at each possible stock price.

Since puts and calls are opposites, our intuition would tell us that the options could not possibly achieve nearly identical returns if you

RISK PROFILE GRAPHS — TWO MONTHS OUT

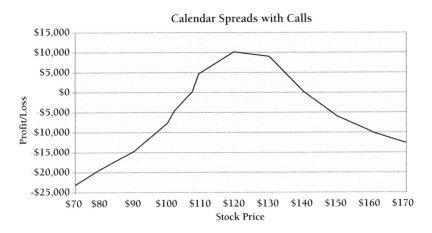

Calendar Spreads with Calls

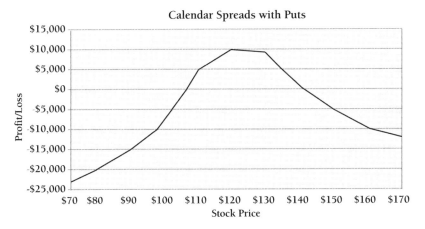

Calendar Spreads with Puts

used either puts or calls. But calendar spreads are entirely different from a strategy of only buying the options.

However, there is a often a major advantage to picking puts over calls. The 30 spreads in the above SHLD example would have cost $24,500 to buy with calls, and only $18,650 with puts. Both charts show a maximum profit of about $10,000 if the stock closes exactly at $120 on expiration, yet the put spreads cost 24% less to place, so the ROI for the puts would be 54% (at the maximum possible gain) compared to 41% if calls were used instead.

At different times, markets value puts and calls differently. If the prevailing outlook of the market is positive (as it is most of the time), call calendar spreads are generally more expensive than the same-strike put calendar spreads. On the other hand, if the general market outlook is negative, put calendar spreads may become more expensive (as they were during most of 2009).

When you buy calendar spreads, you should purchase them at the strike price where you think the stock is headed. If you are bullish about the stock, you buy calendar spreads at strike prices that are higher than the stock price. If you are bearish on a stock, you buy calendar spreads at strike prices that are lower than the stock price. In the *10K Strategy*, we buy calendar spreads that are above, below, and at the stock price to give us protection in both directions — we are not tied to the stock moving in only one direction.

For strike prices that are quite a bit higher than the stock price, it is generally better to buy call calendar spreads rather than put calendar spreads even if they cost a little more. The reason is that the short-term puts are well in the money, and are quite costly. This high price means that they are not traded very actively. With inactively-traded options, a large bid-asked spread usually results. This means that you incur a large bid-asked-spread-penalty when rolling over soon-to-expire put options to the next month out. Sometimes, it is even difficult to roll over these options at a credit.

Appendix C
A NOTE ON EARLY EXERCISE OF SHORT OPTIONS

Should you worry about having your short options exercised?

The short answer is "no." The long answer is also "no."

First-time option traders are often frightened by the specter of someone taking away their stock by exercising an in-the-money call. Many feel that they must maintain a large cash reserve to protect against such an event.

Many of these fears are based on their experience of owning stock and writing calls against the stock — early exercise results in their losing the stock (and incurring a taxable event if their original cost was lower).

In the option market, these fears are unfounded.

The holder of the option is almost always better off selling an option rather than exercising it. For example, if someone owns a soon-to-expire 80 call, and the price of the stock is $81, he could exercise his option and get the stock, making a $1 profit (less what he originally paid for the option, of course). Or he could sell the option for at least $1.50 or more, depending upon how much time there is until expiration. Right up to the last hour, there will be a time premium in that option that he would lose if he exercised rather than sold the option.

Only if you fall asleep or are lost without a phone in Antarctica will you have your stock taken from you when you don't want to.

At least this is true if you are trading options in liquid, (i.e., active) markets. In some inactive option markets, there are inefficiencies. The option market for an inactive stock may be entirely controlled by a single market-maker who is greedy, and not willing to pay a time premium close to expiration. In these markets, it may be necessary for an option holder to exercise to get the price he deserves.

What happens if you are exercised?

§§

In the event that an exercise does take place, you should celebrate! You actually come out better than if you had to buy back the short option. Exercise eliminates the time premium you would have to pay. Your actual net cost is the intrinsic value of the option (the difference between the stock price and the strike price).

So what if you are employing the *10K Strategy*, and you own a call LEAP rather than stock? In this case, your broker will sell (short) enough shares to satisfy the option-owner's desire to get the stock at the strike price. The very next day, you will have short stock in your account as well as the cash the option-exerciser paid to get those shares. You simply buy back the short stock, using the money that was paid to you when you sold it short.

Let's use an example. You have sold 10 July 80 call options short, and the stock is selling at $81 just before expiration. If you bought back these options, they would be selling at just above $1 — let's say $1.25 since there is still time premium in options up until expiration. It would cost you $1250 plus commissions to buy back the options.

If you get exercised, you sell the 1000 shares short for $80 each, or $80,000 less the commission ($15 or less at most discount brokers). You then buy back the 1000 shares in the market for $81, paying $81,000 plus commission. Your net cost was $1000 plus commissions rather than the $1250 plus commissions you would have paid if you had purchased back the options instead.

This works in an IRA as well, even though you are not technically allowed to short stock in an IRA. Your broker will insist that you buy back the short stock on the very next day, however.

Will I lose my LEAPS if my short calls are exercised?

If you are lost in an African jungle on expiration Friday, and your short option is exercised because you do not buy back an in-the-money expiring call option, your broker will still not look to your LEAPS for payment. Instead, the proper number of shares of stock will be sold short in your account, and you will be asked to cover them (buy them back) on Monday.

§§

If you are still lost in the jungle, your broker will buy the short shares back for you on the next trading day before ever considering a sale of your LEAPS (unless you have no other free cash in your account). In short, your LEAPS are safe unless there are no cash or more liquid assets available for the broker to sell! (This is exactly the same position you would be in if exercise had not taken place). Now that I have said this, I must qualify my statement by saying that *thinkorswim* would handle early exercise in this manner. I have heard horror stories from other brokerage firms where they indiscriminately liquidated other positions to cover an early exercise rather than buying back the stock with the cash sitting there. Your broker needs to be options-friendly and savvy.

One caveat. If you are short shares of stock, even for one day, and that day is the ex-dividend day (i.e., the day when owners of the stock are entitled to the dividend), you will be assessed the amount of the dividend. The only time this is likely to be any sort of problem is with the Dow Jones Industrial Average tracking stock (DIA), which pays a monthly dividend, and the ex-dividend date is on expiration Friday. The amount of the dividend is small, so it doesn't hurt much, but needs to be recognized. If you are short an in-the-money call on DIA during expiration week, it would probably be best to buy it back on or before Thursday.

Another ETF that has a dividend that you need to be aware of is SPY, which pays a dividend on the third Friday of March, June, September and December. If you are short an in-the-money call on SPY during expiration week in any of those months, it would be best to buy it back on or before Thursday.

For most stocks, a quarterly dividend is more common, and the ex-dividend date rarely coincides with the expiration date. Furthermore, on the day following an ex-dividend date, the stock usually falls by the amount of the dividend, so when you go to buy shares to cover your short stock, the price will be lower than it would have been before the dividend charge. Once again, the net effect is about the same — whether you buy back the option or are exercised against.

Appendix D
THE TRACK RECORD AT TERRY'S TIPS

erry's Tips has operated sample option portfolios since 2003 for their subscribers to follow or mirror in their own accounts. These portfolios are actual portfolios, and results include all commissions that an investor would pay at *thinkorswim*. Many option newsletters conveniently (for them) do not include commissions in their performance numbers. This makes their results look a lot better than they actually are because commissions are a significant cost of trading options (unlike stock trading which involves much lower commissions).

In 2003, two actual *Terry's Tips* portfolios racked up an 80% average gain for the year. However, 2004 was awful, and most of the previous year's gains were lost. This experience caused a dramatic change in the strategy. With the newly-configured *10K Strategy* in place, we had three consecutive years where the portfolios outperformed the market by a large margin. **In fact, the average gains were over 50% for a 3-year period (2005, 2006, 2007).** However, in the market crash in the fall of 2008 most of our portfolios fell by approximately the same amount as the market in general.

2009 was a difficult year marked by higher-than-usual volatility and a dramatic fall in VIX (the most popular measure of volatility, and consequently, option prices). This experience caused us to modify our strategy once again, and our *Boomer's Revenge* portfolio managed a 60% gain for its first year in business with the new tactics in place.

2010 marked the introduction of Weekly options for many underlying stocks and ETFs, including SPY which is our underlying in 5 of the 8 portfolios currently conducted at *Terry's Tips*. We switched most of the portfolios to trading Weeklys rather than monthlys because we believed that an extraordinary opportunity existed in these options for our basic strategy.

For the first few months of dealing with Weekly options, we were in a learning mode. We made many mistakes trading this new option series, and finally figured out the best way to trade them in late summer of 2010.

Our flagship Weekly portfolio is called the *Weekly Mesa*. It is the only portfolio which was set up to trade Weeklys from its inception. Once we suffered through the learning curve for the new Weeklys, this portfolio gained 114% in the last four months of 2010.

In 2010, we conducted one portfolio using the *Shoot Strategy* (see Appendix E). We used Apple as the underlying. We were lucky. Apple rose 32% during the nine months we operated the portfolio, and our option portfolio gained over 100%.

The best way to get the latest results of these portfolios is to check them out **www.TerrysTips.com/TrackRecord**. Results are updated in the last calendar week of each month.

Cash Withdrawal Policy: For all of our portfolios, the goal is to maintain the portfolios near their "starting" values so that new subscribers can mirror the portfolio at nearly the same initial cost. Cash withdrawals are made from portfolios in increments of 3% of starting portfolio value. This cash withdrawal policy tends to understate the actual annual returns of our portfolios because the money is not left in to earn compound returns in subsequent months. Most of our subscribers roll these cash withdrawals into new "units" of portfolios so that they actually do enjoy the compounding effect.

Summary Statement: We can't promise that we have created the perfect options strategy that achieves extraordinary gains in all kinds of markets, but we are quite proud of our performance for the past few years.

We believe that our results have proved that the *10K Strategy* is just about the best possible investment strategy available to the individual investor.

Remember, options are leveraged securities, and are inherently more risky than conventional investments. Otherwise, the kinds of gains we have achieved in these years would not be possible.

Appendix E
THE SHOOT STRATEGY — AN OPTIONS STRATEGY FOR INDIVIDUAL STOCKS

In spite of the odds against winning, many people seem to like to invest in individual stocks — sort of like picking horses at the race track (and often for similar legitimate selection reasons, like the reputation of the trainer or the jockey or the color of his silks, or the horse's name or his recent race record, or what the touts are touting).

To my way of thinking, picking individual stocks is a whole lot more like gambling than carrying out a prudent option strategy such as the *10K Strategy*. But picking individual stocks is a whole lot easier and a whole lot more fun for many people.

If you insist on picking individual companies, the Shoot Strategy is a better way to make an investment than merely buying the stock. While it is not the *10K Strategy*, it uses the same basic idea — that the decay rate for LEAPS or other long-term options is much less than the decay rate of shorter-term options.

The strategy is outlined in my *White Paper* as the *Shoot for the Stars Strategy*. Les Brown said "Shoot for the moon. Even if you miss, you'll land among the stars. And Confucius said long ago "If you shoot for the stars and hit the moon, it's OK. But you've got to shoot for something. A lot of people don't even shoot."

So we call this the *Shoot Strategy*.

How the Shoot Strategy will perform:

- If the **stock goes up**, the Shoot Strategy will make money. The gain will be considerably greater than the percentage gain would have been if the stock had been bought instead of the LEAPS.
- If the **stock stays flat**, a small gain should result. Since you are collecting slightly more than the average monthly decay of the LEAPS each month (until they have only a few months of remaining life) you will make a small gain. However, even a small gain is more

than you would have made if you had bought the stock and it doesn't go up a penny.

- If the **stock falls**, a loss will usually result just like it would if you had bought the stock, and the loss will likely be a greater percentage loss than if the stock itself had been purchased instead. However, in many cases, the loss could be reduced (or eliminated) if the stock fell during those months when our Trading Rules call for selling in-the-money calls, or if more options were sold than was necessary to recoup the average monthly decay of the LEAPS (this tactic reduces the upside potential gain, however).

An example of the Shoot Strategy:

In late October 2007, *Terry's Tips* used the **www.magicformulainvesting.com** to select 5 companies to demonstrate how the *Shoot Strategy* could work in the real world. We set up a separate demonstration trading account with $5000 for each company. One of the companies was *Accenture Ltd* (ACN). At the time, ACN was trading at $38.40.

We paid $7.70 ($770 plus a $1.50 commission) for each of the 7 LEAPS (Jan-10 40 calls). We calculated that the average monthly decay of our $5,400 worth of LEAPS was about $200 including commissions ($5,400/27 months = $200). Simultaneously with buying the 7 LEAPS, we sold 4 December 40 calls (which would expire worthless a month later) for $155 each, collecting $614 after commissions. Since we sold these calls as a spread at the same time we purchased the LEAPS, we only had to come up with the difference between our cost of $5,400 and our proceeds of $614, or $4,786.

The $614 we collected by selling the December 50 calls comfortably covered the $200 we would be losing for the two months of premium decay on our LEAPS. If the stock stayed absolutely flat for 27 months and we gained $307 each month, we would earn over 50% on our money over that time span even though the stock had not gone up a penny (compare this result to what would have happened if we had purchased the stock instead — absolutely no gain would have been made).

Of course, you probably have figured out that if we sold 5 December 40 calls instead of only 4, we would earn a whole lot more each month. While that is true, if the stock went up strongly, we would not gain nearly as much as we would gain if we had sold only 4 short-term calls. Selling 5 calls instead of only 4 is more similar to the *10K Strategy* (where we are trying to maximize the amount of decay that we collect). In the *Shoot Strategy* we are betting that the stock will go up and the majority of our gains will come from appreciation of the LEAPS we own.

If we had bought $5000 worth of ACN stock, we would have been able to get 130 shares. Our option positions were the equivalent to owning 248 shares of ACN, or almost twice as much as we could have bought with the same money.

Post-Note: Ten months after we started the ACN portfolio, the stock had edged up from $38.40 to $40.51. If we had purchased 130 shares with our $5,000 investment, we would have made a profit of $274 before commissions, or 5.5%.

This compares to a gain of $2,254 that we made in the ACN portfolio using the *Shoot Strategy* (after commissions), or 45.1% on the original $5000 starting value. The *Shoot Strategy* had worked exactly as it was designed. The stock edged up and our return was about 8 times higher than it would have been if we had purchased stock rather than traded the options.

We started 5 different portfolios in October 2007 using the *Shoot Strategy*, each using a different individual stock we had selected from the **www.magicformulainvesting.com** website. Almost two years later, the market in general was down considerably (the S&P 500 had fallen by 31%, the Dow was down 29%, and the Nasdaq was down 25%).

The $25,000 we had invested had eked out a 3% gain during this same period. While this was not much to write home about, it was an extraordinary result compared to the market in general (and presumably just about any mutual fund over the same time period).

Every trade made in all the *Shoot Strategy* portfolios is available for Insiders at **www.TerrysTips.com**. At the time of this writing, we have expanded our list to 6 companies, and replaced some of the early companies with new ones.

General Trading Rules for executing the *Shoot Strategy*:

1) Pick a stock you believe is headed higher (we suggest using **www. magicformulainvesting.com** as a guide — see discussion below).
2) Buy slightly in-the-money call LEAPS. At least two LEAPS must be purchased. If your budget does not warrant buying at least two true LEAPS, shorter-term calls can be purchased as long as they have at least six months of remaining life.
3) Calculate the average monthly decay of the LEAPS (time premium divided by the number of remaining months).
4) Sell enough slightly out-of-the-money current month calls to cover the average monthly decay.
5) A positive net delta must be maintained at all times (i.e., your total option position is long so that if the stock goes up, your investment will gain in value).
6) Near or at expiration, roll over the short calls to the next month (if they are in the money), again selling enough out-of-the-money contracts to cover the average monthly decay. If the expiring calls are out-of-the-money, let them expire worthless and sell the next month out, as above.
7) If short-term calls that have been sold become in the money (i.e., the stock has gone up), they must be bought back during expiration week, and the amount paid must be added to the remaining decay of the LEAPS and a new (higher) average monthly decay bogey established based on the number of remaining months of the LEAPS.

There are a number of other Trading Rules that have proved to be successful for the *Shoot Strategy* , including how to change tactics if the stock should fall, how to adjust which calls to sell during seasonally positive (and negative) months of the year, and the best time to sell the original LEAPS. These important additional Trading Rules are part of the *White Paper* that is included in the *Terry's Tips Insider* service.

Deciding Which Companies to Buy:

The best single source we have found for selecting individual companies is the Magic Formula system outlined in the small book by Joel Greenblat called "The Little Book That Beats the Market" and is available online at **www.magicformulainvesting.com**.

Rather than relying entirely on the Magic Formula, it might be even better to select individual stocks that also rank high at *Investors Business Daily* (IBD), *Value Line*, and by composite analyst rankings. In our opinion, using the *Shoot Strategy* offers considerably higher returns than merely buying the stock, and if you carry it out correctly, you can make money with the *Shoot Strategy* even if the stock falls in value.

Index

1

The real teacher is you.
You're the one who must decide,
of all that comes your way,
what is true and what is not.

— JOHN-ROGER AND PETER MCWILLIAMS,
LIFE 101

Notes

Notes

Notes

SS

Notes